Creating Better Cities with Children and Youth

This manual is dedicated to young people everywhere and those who believe in them.

Creating Better Cities with Children and Youth

A MANUAL FOR PARTICIPATION

DAVID DRISKELL in collaboration with members of the Growing Up in Cities Project

Earthscan Publications Ltd
London and Sterling, VA

UNESCO PUBLISHING

Management of
Social Transformations

First published in the United Kingdom in 2002 by the
United Nations Educational, Scientific and Cultural Organization
and Earthscan Publications Ltd

United Nations Educational, Scientific and Cultural Organization
7, place de Fontenoy, 75007 Paris, France

A catalogue record for this book is available from the British Library

ISBN: 92-3-103815-X (UNESCO)
     1 85383 853 5 (Earthscan)

The authors are responsible for the choice and the presentation of the facts
contained in this book and for the opinions expressed therein, which are not
necessarily those of UNESCO and do not commit the Organization.

The designations employed and the presentation of material throughout this
publication do not imply the expression of any opinion whatsoever on the
part of UNESCO concerning the legal status of any country, territory, city or
area or of its authorities, or the delimitation of its frontiers or boundaries.

Cover design, book design and layout by Dean Driskell
Cover photographs © David Driskell, Robin Moore, Jill Swart-Kruger (front)
and Ilaria Salvadori, David Driskell (back)
Printed and bound in the United Kingdom by Bell & Bain Ltd., Glasgow

For a full list of UNESCO publications please contact:
UNESCO Publishing
7, place de Fontenoy, 75352 Paris 07 SP France
Tel: +33 (0)1 45 68 49 30
Fax: +33 (0)1 45 68 57 41
Email: publishing.promotion@unesco.org
www.unesco.org/publishing

For a full list of Earthscan publications please contact:
Earthscan Publications Ltd
120 Pentonville Road, London, N1 9JN, UK
Tel: +44 (0)20 7278 0433
Fax: +44 (0)20 7278 1142
Email: earthinfo@earthscan.co.uk
www.earthscan.co.uk

22883 Quicksilver Drive, Sterling, VA 20166-2012, USA

Earthscan is an editorially independent subsidiary of Kogan Page Ltd and
publishes in association with WWF-UK and the International Institute for
Environment and Development

This book is printed on elemental chlorine-free paper

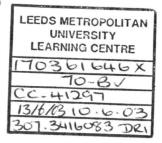

Acknowledgments

Creating Better Cities with Children and Youth represents the collective effort of many people. While I cannot possibly list the names of everyone who has contributed to its development in so many different ways, there are a number of people and organizations who require a special acknowledgment and thanks, for this manual would not exist without their commitment, energy, input and ideas:

• The **UNESCO-MOST Programme** (Management of Social Transformations) for providing the funding that has made this manual possible. In particular, special thanks to *Mr. Pierre Sané,* Assistant Director-General for Social and Human Sciences; *Mr. Ali Kazancigil,* Executive Secretary of the MOST Programme and Director of the Division of Social Science Research and Policy, for his ongoing support of the Growing Up in Cities project; and *Ms. Nadia Auriat,* MOST Programme Specialist, for her hard work, energy and valuable contributions to the ongoing efforts of Growing Up in Cities.

• *Louise Chawla,* who had the vision which sparked the current Growing Up in Cities effort, for bringing together a dynamic group of people to work on the project; and for her tireless coordination and constant encouragement. She is the glue that has held the project together these past years.

• All of the project team members who implemented the 1996/97 Growing Up in Cities effort around the globe and whose ideas and experiences provided the basis for this manual: *Nilda Cosco* and *Robin Moore* in Argentina; *Karen Malone, Beau Beza* and *Lindsay Hasluck* in Australia; *Kanchan Bannerjee, S. Kandaswami, S.R. Prakash, B. Radha,* and *Sowmya Reddy* in India; *Hanne Wilhjelm* in Norway; *Krystyna Skarzynska* and *Piotr Olaf Zylicz* in Poland; *Jill Swart-Kruger, Peter Rich, Melinda Swift, Nondumiso Mabuza* and the rest of their team in South Africa; *Barry Percy-Smith* in the UK, and *Ilaria Salvadori* in the USA, and all of those at all of the sites whom I did not have the opportunity to meet in person. It is no exaggeration for me to say they are one of the finest groups I have ever had the pleasure of working with. This manual is the product of their collective effort.

• The many other funding agencies that made Growing Up in Cities a reality around the globe, especially those agencies which provided funding for the project's start-up and general coordination, including: the **Norwegian Centre for Child Research**; the **Norwegian Ministry of Child and Family Affairs**; **Childwatch International**; and the **MOST Programme of UNESCO**. Support for individual sites came from a variety of sources, including **UNICEF** and **UNESCO-South Africa**; the **International Development Research Centre of Canada**; the **Jacobs Foundation** of Switzerland; the **October Foundation** of Argentina; the **Nene University College** Northampton, UK; **North Carolina State University**, USA; the **FAAR Foundation** (Fondazione Architetto Augusto Rancilio) of Italy; the **Housing Bank of Norway**; the **Norwegian Agency for Development** (NORAD); and the **Human Sciences Research Councils** of South Africa and Australia. Funding for implementation of environmental improvements in South Africa, Argentina, and India was granted by the **Children's Hour Helping Fund** of NRK, the Norwegian broadcasting company.

• The **MOST Programme of UNESCO**, the **Averroès European Training Centre for Early Child Development and the Family** and the **Dutch Ministry of Health, Welfare, and Sports** for their generous support of the Creating Better Cities with Children and Youth international training workshops in The Netherlands in 1997/1998, which contributed to development of this manual. Special thanks to the Averroès Project Managers for International Training, *Joyce Cordus* and *Karin Reijnders,* for their hard work in making the training workshops a success, and to all the participants for their energy, input, and commitment to young people's participation.

• *Gillian Whitcomb,* chief of the Publications Unit of **UNESCO's Social and Human Sciences Sector**, for her patience, insights, humor and intellect, and to those who have reviewed and given feedback on this manual at its various stages of development, including *Louise Chawla, Robin Moore, Hanne Wilhjelm, Karen Malone, Roger Hart* and the reviewers and editorial staff at **Earthscan** — their time and input has been extremely helpful and very much appreciated.

• The late *Kevin Lynch,* who provided the inspiration and direction for the first Growing Up in Cities project in the 1970s. His passion and intellect as a planner and human being continue to improve the quality of our cities even now.

• *Dean Driskell,* who has transformed my clumsy word processing into a beautifully designed book, once again convincing me that he is a graphic design genius as well as a great brother.

• My partner and best friend, *Neema Kudva,* who has contributed her ideas, time, energy, and support to make this manual a reality; *Kieran* and *Mira,* who help us see the world and ourselves in new ways; and my parents, who taught me the value and importance of community participation in their words and deeds.

• And most of all, *the many young people and other community members at all of the Growing Up in Cities sites* who gave of their time and energy to teach us about their communities, their lives, and ourselves.

David Driskell

Contents

1 First Steps

2 Young People's Participation

3 Organizing a Project

4 Designing the Process

5 Getting Under Way

6 Participation Toolkit

7 Making Change Happen

Appendices

Foreword

Children and youth are seldom involved in the construction of their environment. They are considered too inexperienced, too unrealistic, too unqualified. Yet their fresh perspectives may be exactly what is needed to see clearly into the realm of new possibilities. It is my strong conviction that tapping into young people's ideas and reflections is essential to improving our cities. *Creating Better Cities with Children and Youth* can help us move in that direction.

This manual is the culmination of a remarkable international project that first began twenty-six years ago under UNESCO's Man and the Biosphere Programme, and then re-emerged six years ago under the auspices of UNESCO's Social and Human Sciences Sector. It suggests how to create an atmosphere of trust between youth and adults in order for real communication to take place. It shows ways of assisting young people to be heard by those who are in positions to make official policy decisions that affect the quality of their lives. It is a guide on how to access children's knowledge — both intuitive and based on experience — that is so often repressed or lost, yet that can be a precious insight into their daily realities and a powerful lever for improvement of urban life.

In taking the time to explore and apply the methods that have been developed in this research project, you will be sensitized to new ways of approaching poverty reduction and environmental design projects. You will also discover methods for involving local officials in such a way that they will remember to listen to all sub-groups in their population, particularly children and youth, and to include them in developing policies.

As a person continuously devoted to the compliance and enforcement of all human rights — civil, cultural, economic, political and social — I feel particularly committed to the guidance contained in this volume — guidance that encourages patience, perseverance and hope.

Putting into practice the methods described in *Creating Better Cities with Children and Youth* can help ensure that children's rights are respected. I am therefore proud to offer it to the international community, with the firm belief that it can contribute to making this world a better place for current and future generations of children and youth.

Pierre Sané
ASSISTANT DIRECTOR-GENERAL FOR
SOCIAL AND HUMAN SCIENCES, UNESCO

Introductory Note

Throughout the development debate over the past ten years, there has been an increasing realization of the need to generate participation of vulnerable populations in the design and implementation of projects that affect them. An accompanying trend has been the new emphasis on the importance of creating local ownership over development initiatives so as to maximise their success. These two concepts, and the growing understanding of what 'works and doesn't work' in national planning initiatives, represent a step toward adopting a rights-based approach to development, and toward the twin goals of poverty reduction and increased equality and social cohesion.

However, a number of questions remain. For example, what constitutes genuine participation — and not tokenism — particularly when we are talking about the participation of children and youth? How can development practitioners, municipalities, local non-governmental organizations and other committed actors design authentic participatory projects in a situation of often limited resources? How do the concepts of participation and ownership respond to international declarations and conventions, such as the United Nations Convention on the Rights of the Child; the Universal Declaration on Human Rights; the Convention on the Protection of Migrant Workers and their Families; and the United Nations Resolution (May 2001) stating that the prevalence of extreme poverty is a fundamental human rights violation? How can governments undertake steps to ensure that the principles enshrined within these Conventions and Declarations are part and parcel of integrated, sector-wide programming and resource distribution?

Young people are generally ignored or simply not incorporated in many instances of project design. This contravenes Article 12 of the Convention on the Rights of the Child, and it represents a sorely short-sighted view: it is these young people who constitute the very wealth of a country's future, and investments must be made in providing them a chance to participate actively and genuinely in social, environmental and political decision-making. Too often, when interviewing young people, one gets the response: *No one listens to me. The politicians don't care. Nobody cares.* It is precisely this impression that can be changed through careful methods designed specifically for working with young people. This is what *Creating Better Cities with Children and Youth* is all about.

This manual is the fruit of a UNESCO supported participatory research project within the Management of Social Transformations (MOST) programme, which provides an international platform for supporting high quality comparative, interdisciplinary and policy-relevant research. The purpose of the Growing Up in Cities project is to work with children and youth in different countries in order to gain insight into how young people feel about the quality of their physical environment and their priorities for change. It seeks to discover how — if at all — they are consulted by people in authority on the variety of urban planning decisions that inevitably affect their lives, and how they can succeed in influencing local urban policy. The companion book to this manual, entitled *Growing up in an Urbanising World*[1], provides a description and analysis of projects in eight countries, and includes revealing insights by the young people on their environment and on their lives.

Creating Better Cities with Children and Youth builds on that research, and provides readers with compelling arguments as to how ignoring young people's views jeopardizes the social, economic and environmental quality of our communities and neighbourhoods. It shows how empowering young people by including them in local initiatives can create feelings of solidarity and respect for one's environment, for public institutions and for the public authorities that run them and serve them.

This manual is markedly different from other existing manuals and training material on participation in a number of respects:

- It is based on a rigorous comparative research methodology — not on one-shot intervention research — with work undertaken in sites in a variety of countries including Argentina, Australia, India, Lebanon, Norway, Papua New Guinea, Poland, South Africa, Sweden, the United Kingdom and the United States.
- It is anchored in the views and responses received from the children and youth who took time to work with the research facilitators.
- It is a user-friendly, comprehensive tool that will assist in the development of participatory projects with children and youth. It explains in clear language various methods that can be used, the pitfalls to be avoided, and the arguments as to why this is a just and necessary approach to environmental design and development.
- It goes beyond helping in the preparation of participatory projects: it shows how young participants can design and implement local improvements, illustrating this with examples from the Growing Up in Cities project.

- Finally, it has been made possible only through the incredible drive, advocacy, teamwork and international understanding of all those who have contributed to this project. International work is often costly. The generosity and dedication of the team members assisted us in overcoming the numerous obstacles in supporting international research.

There is an array of talented persons who deserve to be acknowledged for their contribution to this work.

First and foremost, the author of this volume, David Driskell, who has not only done extensive research but has invested significant time in reviewing masses of material and reworking it into the product that you now see. As a firm believer in participatory processes, he has been a wonderful team leader for this manual. His capacity to organize the material, present it in a clear and friendly fashion, and communicate it with his warm writing skill have made this volume a special contribution to the work on participation, urban design and the rights of the child. The investment he has made in this work is an investment for children and youth around the world. We at UNESCO are very grateful for his dedication to this project.

Dean Driskell, the designer, has been able to turn a mass of information into a wonderfully structured manual, greatly increasing its user-friendliness. A true magician. Our appreciation is extended to him for his time and effort.

Louise Chawla, the unfailing, dynamic team leader for the entire international Growing Up in Cities project has been the motor, support and drive behind this international project. Her competence, experience, generosity and optimism are the key elements behind its success.

All the contributors (they are named individually by the author in his acknowledgement) have been a source of inspiration and professional satisfaction to me. It is

---

[1] Chawla, Louise (Ed.) Growing up in an Urbanising World, UNESCO Publishing/Earthscan, 2002

rare to have the privilege to work with such an international group. On behalf of UNESCO, I extend to each and every one of them our gratitude. It is projects like this that breathe life into the work of the UN System.

Roger Hart and Sheridan Bartlett of the Children's Environments Research Group of The City University of New York, and David Satterthwaite of the Urban Settlement Programme of the International Institute for Environment and Development. We are grateful to them for their encouragement and assistance.

Within UNESCO, there are a number of people whom I would like to acknowledge.

First, I would like to thank Dr. Ali Kazancigil, Director of the Division for Social Science Research and Policy, for having supported this project over the years. He has been a valuable partner for all of us in this work, and has constantly stood behind the team and the objectives of the Growing Up in Cities project from which this manual emerges. His unfailing confidence in the quality of this project has been appreciated by all, and we are very grateful.

Philippe Ratte, planning officer for the Sector of Social and Human Sciences, has been a dedicated and supportive colleague, always lending a helping hand in time of need. He has provided constant professional and intellectual support to this project. I wish to express my gratitude for his defence of the principles and objectives that comprise it.

Gillian Whitcomb is our lifeline to publishing. Her professionalism and publishing skills have greatly facilitated putting this volume together. On behalf of the Growing Up in Cities team, I wish to thank her for what I know were often long nights and working weekends to meet tight deadlines. I would also like to thank Jennifer Moate for her perspicacious comments and enthusiasm.

Brigitte Colin, architect and colleague, has given her unfailing support and encouragement to this work, and enriched the conceptual framework with her extensive international experience in including vulnerable populations in landscape architecture and spatial design programmes initiated by municipalities. We thank her and look forward to continued cooperation.

Finally, on behalf of UNESCO, we express our gratitude to all the children and youth who have made this volume possible. As the methods and objectives of this publication are disseminated to other sites in the world, we hope that municipalities, non-governmental organizations and United Nations Agencies will recognize the valuable contribution these young people have made toward improving our common heritage for all future generations.

Nadia Auriat
UNESCO PROGRAMME SPECIALIST

About this Manual

As support for young people's participation in community development grows — and it has significantly in recent years — questions like "Is young people's participation really worthwhile?" are heard less and less, and questions like "What methods are proven to be effective?" are heard more and more.

Creating Better Cities with Children and Youth is a direct and detailed response to the latter type of question. It devotes some space to the principles and concepts of young people's participation, but focuses on field-tested approaches and methods for actually making it happen.

Apart from involving young people in making improvements to the places where they live, one of the most effective strategies for creating better cities is through the actual process of participation: helping young people to listen to one another, to respect differences of opinion, and to find common ground; developing their capacities for critical thinking, evaluation and reflection; supporting their processes of discovery, awareness building, and collective problem-solving; and helping them develop the knowledge and skills for making a difference in their world.

I hope this manual will be a useful tool for those of you who share these beliefs, and that it will help you to realize the potential that exists in the simple yet powerful act of listening to young people's voices and engaging them in processes of constructive community change.

OVERVIEW

Creating Better Cities with Children and Youth is a practical manual on how to conceptualize, structure and facilitate the participation of young people in community development. It is intended for use by urban planners, municipal officials, community development staff, non-governmental organizations, educators, youth-serving agencies, youth advocates, and others who are involved in community development: for everyone who feels concern for young people and the quality of their lives, and who believes in the value of community education and empowerment as the foundation of a vibrant and resilient civil society.

This manual provides a framework for planning participatory projects and building institutional and political support for implementation. It outlines the necessary steps for organizing a participatory project, and shows how young people can be engaged in analysing and prioritizing their needs and implementing appropriate responses.

The manual's core ideas and methods have been field-tested in a wide range of urban settings in both developing and industrialized cities through the work of the Growing Up in Cities project (see page 19). Examples from project sites help to illustrate the methods and demonstrate how they can be customized to local needs. They also highlight the universal applicability and value of young people's participation and provide lessons and insights to help ensure a successful project.

HOW TO USE THE MANUAL

Here are tips for how to get the most out of this manual:

Familiarize yourself with the basic concepts. *Chapters 1 and 2* present basic concepts about youth participation in community development — why it is important, what benefits it has, and what factors should be considered when trying to develop a youth participation programme. If this is a new area of interest for you, spend time reviewing the information in these chapters, and review the list of books, documents, videos and online resources in Appendix B.

Determine how much work is needed to 'get started.' *Chapter 3* discusses the logistical issues in putting together a participatory project. If you already have a project or programme in place, you may not need to spend much time on this chapter. But if you are starting from scratch, this chapter should be studied carefully. A quick review of the checklist at the beginning of the chapter should help determine how much of this chapter is relevant to you.

Develop a logical sequence of methods. A successful participation programme leads participants together through a sequence of activities and events that allows them to explore issues, develop and evaluate alternatives, and take action. *Chapter 4* provides an approach for thinking about the overall process design to ensure an effective programme.

Do what it takes to ensure success. Making participation 'work' requires more than simply going out in the field and talking with young people. You need to make sure that all project staff are appropriately trained, that there is a high level of comfort and trust between participants and staff, that ethical issues are understood and respected, and that the basics of daily project management are taken care of (i.e. there is good communication between team members, consent forms are filled out, field notes and materials are properly filed, etc.). *Chapter 5* covers these issues.

Choose and customize methods according to your needs. The 'Participation Toolkit' in *Chapter 6* provides an overview of basic methods that can be used to facilitate young people's participation. But it is not a cookbook! There are no magic recipes for meaningful participation. You need to select the methods that are appropriate for your needs, and customize them accordingly. Use the information as a starting point, and then create your own method variations and ideas.

Always maximize participation. Throughout the process, tap into the resources and knowledge of your local community — especially children and youth. Share the manual and its ideas with them, and facilitate a group process of creative innovation.

Use the manual as a training tool. This manual was developed as a training resource as well as a field guide. Use it to train your staff, young people, and community residents about what participation is, why it is important, and how young people can become effective participants in community development. The methods in *Chapter 6* have been written and designed so that they can be used for field training and group discussions.

Focus on action. Ensure that every participation programme leads to some form of action in response to the input and ideas of the participants — with the participants involved in deciding upon and implementing the action. An 'action' does not have to be grand in scale to be meaningful. *Chapter 7* provides examples of how evaluation results can be translated into action programmes.

Build networks of support and share your ideas. Join with others who are interested in or involved in projects that promote young people's participation. Work together to support each other's efforts, share ideas, and develop local resources. The Growing Up in Cities project has a network of groups and individuals working to promote young people's participation. For information regarding members in your area and current network activities, contact Growing Up in Cities (*www.unesco.org/most/growing.htm*).

About the Growing Up in Cities Project

Growing Up in Cities is an international effort to better understand how urban children and youth perceive, use and value their local environment, and how that environment can encourage or inhibit their development as individuals and fellow citizens. Foremost among the project's goals is to encourage the participation of young people in research and evaluation processes as well as in actions to improve the communities in which they live.

Project Background

The contemporary Growing Up in Cities project was conceived within the Children and Environment Program of the Norwegian Centre for Child Research, Trondheim, Norway, in 1994. When the project was initiated, the goal was to replicate and extend the classic UNESCO project of the same name (originated in the 1970s under the direction of Kevin Lynch at the Massachusetts Institute of Technology, Boston, USA).

While many of the project's goals remain the same as they were in the 1970s, there has been an important shift towards a more participatory and action-oriented approach. This is due in part to the policies that now exist at the international level and to growing support for participatory, democratic approaches to development. It is also due to more widespread and severe urban problems that are impacting children's lives in increasingly negative

and visible ways, challenging us to do more than just understand what is happening. We need to take action. Most importantly, the strong participatory orientation of the contemporary Growing Up in Cities project is due to the increasing demand among local communities to be heard and involved in the decisions that affect them.

1996/97 Project Sites and Results

In 1996/97, the Growing Up in Cities project was renewed in the original sites of Melbourne, Australia, and Warsaw, Poland; and new sites were established in Buenos Aires, Argentina; Johannesburg, South Africa; Bangalore, India; Northampton, UK; Oakland, California, USA; and Trondheim, Norway. While each site undertook the same set of core research methods, the renewed emphasis on participation and action has resulted in extended projects that vary significantly between sites, particularly in the actions that have come out of the initial research activities. The results of the 1996/97 projects are summarized in *Growing Up in an Urbanising World* (see Resources list in Appendix B).

The work completed at the 1996/97 project sites and subsequent experiences at various training workshops and new site locations have also served as the testing ground for the approach and methods presented in this manual.

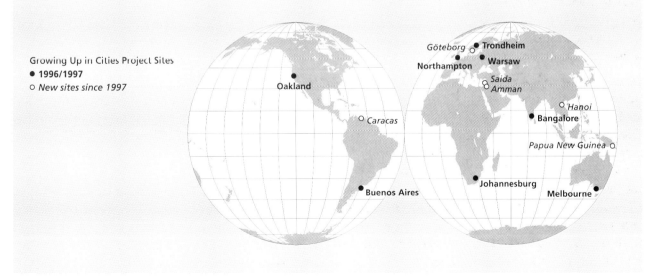

Growing Up in Cities Project Sites
● **1996/1997**
○ *New sites since 1997*

First Steps

CHAPTER ONE

A child in Buenos Aires, Argentina, gives a tour of her neighbourhood, showing where she goes and the things she likes and dislikes.

© ROBIN MOORE

We have not yet made this city what it could be or should be just by painting some houses and planting some gardens for free…we have created hope that didn't exist before. We know what the future could be and we have the desire to make it come into being.

JULIA POINTER, Youth Volunteer, Detroit Summer [1]

This manual is a tool to help you to design and implement projects that involve young people as partners in the community development process. Ultimately, its goal is to improve the quality of young people's lives as well as the quality of the places where they live.

Achieving this goal will require commitment, energy, patience and resilience. In the end, as well as along the way, it will be a rewarding journey with valuable results.

This chapter outlines the essential ideas on which the manual is based, and the factors that help to make cities good places — or not such good places — for young people. These first steps, which culminate with an evaluation of your own city as a place for young people (at the end of this chapter), will help to establish a framework for what lies ahead.

Starting Points

why you should involve them.

Young people are valuable members of the community, both now and in the future.
Young people represent a significant portion (if not the majority) of most urban populations. They are affected in both the short and long term by today's decisions and actions. They will also be important actors in the local community for many years to come. Investments made in developing their knowledge, skills and social responsibility are the best investments we can make towards creating a better future.

The local environment can help, or hinder, young people's development.
The local environment encompasses all those factors that contribute to an area's uniqueness as a place, including its physical, social, economic, political and historical characteristics. It can pose significant threats to young people's physical, mental, emotional and social development, or it can provide positive development opportunities for them to explore, grow and engage with the world, helping to develop valuable skills as well as self-identity and self-confidence. While the local environment is not the only factor in young people's development, it is often an overlooked and underappreciated factor. Planners, designers and managers of cities must understand the impact that development decisions have on young people's lives.

Global initiatives require local implementation.
The United Nations Convention on the Rights of the Child (1989) and other important UN initiatives such as Agenda 21 and the Habitat (UN Centre for Human Settlements) Agenda have established a global policy framework in support of sustainable cities and participatory development practices. While this global framework provides critical policy support, change in the local environment and in young people's lives must be implemented at the local level. If the lofty goals set forth by these global initiatives are to be realized, we must support real change in local policy and practice.

Local research and knowledge are the foundation for policy and action.
Policy-making, development decisions and other actions are too often based on an inadequate or inaccurate understanding of the local situation. This is especially true when dealing with children and youth in complex urban environments. The world of urban childhood today is changing rapidly, and the complexities of today's cities do not lend themselves to simplistic generalizations. Policies and actions that respond to community issues must be based on a thorough understanding of those issues and their context. Quality research that draws upon local knowledge is an essential first step in effective policy-making.

Young people should be partners in community development.
Young people should be considered as legitimate participants — along with other groups in the community — in the development process. They are intimately familiar with the local environment and are the most knowledgeable on how the local environment and development decisions impact on their lives. They should be active and valued partners in efforts towards positive community change.

Everybody learns and grows through young people's participation.
Young people's participation in community development is a powerful vehicle for social transformation. Through participatory community evaluation, planning, design and management, they are exposed to a wide range of people and ideas, and develop valuable new skills. Adult professionals, government officials and local decision-makers also grow and learn through participation, developing a more comprehensive and accurate understanding of local issues and a greater appreciation of the perspectives and insights of young citizens.

Creating better cities will require a multi-tier, long-term approach.
The creation of urban environments that truly support children's development must address a wide range of issues at the local, national and global levels. While no single project will magically result in an urban environment that meets young people's needs, each will be an important step in the right direction, affecting change not only in the physical environment, but also in the lives of those who participate in bringing about change, and creating opportunities to move on to new issues.

Physical environmental issues and actions provide a good starting point.
The physical environment is multi-sensory, real and concrete. This makes it easier to understand than more abstract policy issues. Young people's experience in transforming the physical environment

— seeing real change that is a direct result of their own initiatives — can be a valuable exercise in community empowerment. It is an important step on the road to greater structural and systemic change in the creation of sustainable, healthy and liveable cities.

Places that are better for young people are better for everyone.
When a city, town, neighbourhood or suburban area becomes a better place for young people to live, it becomes a better place for everyone. A more humane, people-supportive environment is in everyone's interest.

What Makes a City a Good Place for Young People?

How do we determine whether a city does or does not support human development? What makes a city a good place in which to grow up?

The following is a list of child-generated indicators of a good place, based on young people's own evaluations of their local communities.[2]

- **Social integration.** Young people feel welcome throughout the community, and interact with other age groups in public and semi-public places. They have a sense of belonging and of being valued.

Young people express satisfaction with their communities when there are high levels of social integration, strong community and cultural identity, extended family and peer networks, access to green spaces, and a variety of interesting activity settings.

© ROBIN MOORE

© HANNE WILHJELM

- **Variety of interesting activity settings.** There is a variety of places for young people, including places where they can meet friends, talk or play informal games; play sports; join in community work; shop and run errands; be alone or away from adult supervision; and observe action on the street or similar public places.

- **Safety and freedom of movement.** There is a general sense of safety, even in areas where crime exists, because young people are familiar with the local area and its adult residents, with whom they interact regularly. Because there is a sense of safety, young people are able to move about to meet friends and find interesting things to do.

- **Peer meeting places.** Young people are able to claim corners and niches in the community as their own, where they can play and socialize — a street corner, a place in a local park or plaza, a coffee shop or store, a playing field, a community centre or an empty plot.

- **Cohesive community identity.** Young people are aware of their community's history and take pride in its accomplishments. They are active participants in its festivals and cultural life.

- **Green areas.** Green space is accessible to young people in some form, from flat green fields for organized sports to tree-shaded parks and safe overgrown 'wild' areas.

NEGATIVE CHARACTERISTICS

At the other end of the spectrum, negative characteristics were identified in communities where young people voiced a sense of alienation about their local environment. These negative indicators include:

- **Stigma and social exclusion.** Young people feel unwanted and left out. They do not mix with other age groups, are not seen in public places, and are not allowed to gather with their peers due to either official or unofficial policy. Local media often focus their reporting on 'youth problems' and adults voice mistrust and suspicion of young people.

- **Boredom.** Places that are set aside for young people are often so sterile, featureless or littered that young people avoid them.

- **Fear of harassment and crime.** Young people avoid specific areas or whole sections of the community due to fear of harassment and violence. Thus, even though interesting places might be nearby, they are not accessible.

- **Racial or ethnic tension.** Young people experience fear and stigmatization based on their race or ethnic origin.

- **Heavy traffic.** Streets and other public places are taken over by cars — moving and parked — so that little space is left for people. High speed and high volume of traffic make even the places adjacent to streets unpleasant and unsafe, and create major barriers to children's movement in the local community.

- **Uncollected rubbish and litter.** Young people see littered parks and streets in their area as ugly in themselves and as signs of neglect.
- **Lack of basic services.** The lack of basic services such as water, sewerage and waste collection results in more work for young people (such as fetching water) as well as the indignity and shame of being dirty. It also increases the prevalence of disease.
- **Sense of political powerlessness.** Young people doubt the value of their ideas and opinions, and are sceptical about adults taking them seriously. These sentiments are often reflected in the community at large, in doubts about the community's ability to create positive change, and scepticism about politicians and the political system.

Public spaces that have been taken over by cars create unsafe and undesirable places for young people.

Is *My* City a Good Place for Young People?

What do the young people in *my* city feel about the place where they live? Do they feel valued as members of the community? Are there places for them to meet with their friends? Do they participate in community activities? Do they feel safe? *Is my city a good place in which to grow up?*

These questions are probably foremost in your mind as you begin to use this manual, followed closely by, *What can I do to make my city a better place in which to grow up?*

Traditional methods for determining the answers to these questions have relied on quantitative measures of children's life quality, such as infant mortality rates, literacy, income levels, housing density, traffic flows and crime statistics. These measures have provided valuable statistical indicators that allow different cities to be compared and changes tracked over time. But do they tell us whether a city is one in which children can grow and develop to the full extent of their powers?

To truly understand the lives of young people, it is necessary to go beyond statistical measures. Young people themselves must have the opportunity to voice their perspectives, and to translate their ideas and energies into positive change.

Self-Evaluation of Your City as a Place for Young People

Do *you* think your city is a good place in which to grow up? What do you think are the most positive features of your city, from a young person's perspective? What do you think are the least positive features?

To help you compare your own evaluation of your city with young people's evaluations, we suggest that you make an initial assessment using the worksheet on the following page. Later, after working with young people in the local area and seeing the city through their eyes, revisit your initial assessment. Were there things identified by young people that did not appear on your list? Did they emphasize issues that did not seem so important to you? Did you include issues that young people did not see themselves?

Use your self-evaluation later in the process to discuss how your views have changed over the course of the project, and to engage young people in a discussion about how their own views may have changed as a result of their interactions during the project.

© BARRY PERCY-SMITH

ENDNOTES

1 Myrna Margulies Breitbart, 'Dana's Mystical Tunnel: Young People's Designs for Survival and Change in the City', in Tracey Skelton and Gil Valentine (eds.), *Cool Places: Geographies of Youth Cultures,* (London: Routledge, 1998), p. 325.

2 Adapted from Louise Chawla (ed.), *Growing Up in an Urbanising World,* Paris/London, UNESCO Publishing/Earthscan, 2002.

WORKSHEET

Self-evaluation of your city as a place for young people

	POSITIVE ATTRIBUTES	NEGATIVE ATTRIBUTES
Social Integration Do young people feel welcome throughout the community? Do they interact with other age groups in public places and in formal or informal activities? Do they have a sense of belonging and of being valued?		
Gathering Places and Activity Settings Are there a variety of places for young people to meet friends, talk, play sports or informal games, shop, be alone, or just 'hang out'?		
Safety and Freedom of Movement Is there a general sense of safety? Are young people familiar with the local area? Are they able to move around the community freely on their own, without fear or concerns about their safety?		
Access to Nature Do young people have access to natural settings? Are there trees to climb? Fields for organized sports? Developed parks and play areas? 'Wild areas' where they can explore on their own?		

	POSITIVE ATTRIBUTES	NEGATIVE ATTRIBUTES
Community Image and Identity Do residents in general, and young people in particular, have a positive opinion about where they live? Are they aware of its history and proud of its accomplishments? Do they participate in community activities and cultural life?		
Land Tenure Do residents own the land and structures in which they live? Do they have undisputed legal title? Are there any threats of relocation or displacement from authorities or private developers/landowners?		
Basic Goods and Services Do residents have secure access to food, water, shelter and sanitation?		
Local Power and Control Does the local community have a sense of control over its destiny? Do they feel a stake in local decision-making and have a say in political outcomes? Are young people involved in the decision-making process? Do they have hope about the future?		

Young People's Participation

CHAPTER TWO

Children meet with adults
in Johannesburg, South
Africa, to discuss the day's
participation activities.

© MELINDA SWIFT

*The darkness can never swallow a lamp. Even the tiniest lamp
lights up the dark in however small a way.*

SUNDERLAL BANUGUNA[1]

The popularity of participatory planning has grown substantially in recent years, with support from a wide range of international agencies, national governments and non-governmental organizations (NGOs). While previously considered a revolutionary idea, today citizen participation in community development is widely accepted, and support for the participation of young people continues to grow.

However, despite the rhetoric that is reflected in many speeches, reports and project proposals, the realities of citizen participation are often misunderstood (particularly the participation of young people) and the practice of participation is often misdirected, applied in inappropriate ways, or controlled and manipulated for purposes that are at odds with the interests of local communities.

This chapter provides a basic definition of what we mean when we talk about 'participation', both in general terms and specifically as it relates to young people. This basic understanding of what participation is — and what it is not — provides the essential foundation for any participatory planning programme.

What is Participation?

In general terms, participation is about local communities being actively involved in the decisions that affect them. It is 'a fundamental right of citizenship...the means by which a democracy is built and...a standard against which democracies should be measured'.[2]

Participation shifts the focal point of planning and decision-making towards people at the local level who are most affected by the decisions being made. It is based on the beliefs that (a) development must, first and foremost, be in the interest of local residents, including young people; (b) people who live in the area being planned have the most intimate knowledge of the area and its issues (and young people have knowledge and perspectives that are different from those of adults); and (c) the people who will be most affected by decisions have most at stake and therefore have the right to participate in making those decisions. Meaningful participation involves residents of all ages in evaluating the local area and identifying issues, reviewing and analysing relevant data, considering alternative courses of action, developing consensus on the best plan of action to take, and putting the plan into practice.

Participation is 'a fundamental right of citizenship... The means by which a democracy is built and...a standard against which democracies should be measured.'

PARTICIPATION IS...

- **Local.** While participatory development may be promoted on a regional, national or even international scale, its implementation is intrinsically local. It is focused on and tailored to the needs and issues of the local community. 'Outsiders' may play a role as facilitators, animators or technical specialists, but they are there to listen to and provide support to the local community; not to dictate solutions or preconceived outcomes based on their own biases or perspectives.

- **Transparent.** The aims of participatory projects are clear to all the participants. Outside experts involved in participatory projects — including local municipal officials, sponsoring agencies, development professionals, advocacy organizations and others — are clear about who they are, what they are doing there, and what can and cannot be expected of them.

- **Inclusive.** Participatory processes should be accessible to all members of the community, regardless of age, gender, race or ethnic background, religion, disability or socio-economic status. The critical question for any participatory project is not so much who participated, but who did not, and why.

- **Interactive.** Participation is about local residents having a voice as well as listening to the other voices in their community — including the voices of young people. Participatory development is a community-wide dialogue, with adults and young people working together.

One of the most critical skills for a successful participation programme: the ability to listen.

- **Responsive.** Because the process responds to local needs and conditions, every process is different. While there may be consistency in the general approach, the exact sequence of steps is never the same. Facilitators are flexible and respond to changing needs and conditions, relying on their own best judgement rather than a rigid set of rules to determine the best course of action at any point in time. Sponsoring agencies and professionals are willing to give participation the time that it needs, knowing that it cannot be rushed. Time is allowed for everyone to voice opinions, listen to others, explore and analyse issues and alternatives, and formulate and carry out plans of action. This is a particularly important principle in relation to young people's participation.

- **Relevant.** Participation builds on local knowledge — the information and insights that local residents have about the area where they live and the issues that affect their lives. It acknowledges and values the input and perceptions of young people, which are often very different from those of adults. It also brings in information and specialized skills from outside the community to ensure an informed process. Technical information and abstract concepts are presented in accessible terms and formats that can be easily understood by local residents, including young people.

- **Educational.** Participatory development is a learning process for everyone, including project sponsors, local officials, project staff and area residents of all ages. If participation is to succeed, all participants must be willing to learn, change attitudes and forge new ways of understanding. For young people, participation is a vehicle for building their capacities in environmental evaluation, group problem-solving and democratic decision-making — valuable project outcomes in addition to whatever else the project hopes to achieve.

- **Reflective.** Participatory development places considerable emphasis on the role of reflection as an opportunity for individual and group learning. Through reflection, participants identify what worked well (both in terms of the process and its outcomes) as well as what could be improved. This often leads the group to identify larger issues that may be affecting the local area or their group process, raising their level of awareness and leading to new avenues of group action.

- **Transformative.** The ultimate goal of participatory development is some form of transformation in the local community. This transformation is not limited to physical and economic changes, but also encompasses changes in the relationship between the local community and the society at large; changes in the relationships between participants; and (perhaps most important) changes in the personal values and perceptions of everyone involved. For young people, this transformative process can be quite profound, helping to shape their personal value system and developing their expertise as informed, active and responsible citizens.

- **Sustainable.** If local residents support a project and feel that it responds to their needs, they are more likely to participate in its implementation and ongoing management, thereby supporting project sustainability. In a larger sense, sustainable development can only be achieved through participation, as it fosters local skills and capacities as well as a strong sense of personal responsibility and commitment to action. Through participation, local communities — including children and youth — define and develop a stewardship role towards the local environment, understanding how their own action, or inaction, impacts on long-term environmental quality.

- **Personal.** Participation is a process of human interaction. Its success is largely determined by the attitudes, values and skills of the individuals, organizations and communities involved. Adults who work with young people in a participatory process must be able to give over control to young participants; be perceptive and sensitive to their needs; be open-minded; be willing to listen and learn; and be transparent. Perhaps most important, they need to be genuinely concerned about the interests of young people, and committed to working with them to make positive changes in their lives.

- **Voluntary.** Participation is never a requirement. People engage in a participatory process because they appreciate the importance of the issue, understand the ways in which they can be involved, and believe that their participation will make a difference.

The Benefits of Young People's Participation

A commitment to young people's participation in community development requires understanding what participation is, and appreciating the potential benefits for everyone involved.

BENEFITS FOR YOUNG PEOPLE

- Participate in a new and exciting activity.
- Look at and understand their local community and environment in new ways.
- Learn about democracy and tolerance.
- Develop a network of new friends, including community role models and resource people.
- Develop new skills and knowledge.
- Help create positive change in the local environment and other aspects of the community.
- Develop a sense of environmental stewardship and civic responsibility.
- Develop confidence in their abilities to accomplish the goals they set.
- Strengthen their self-esteem, identity and sense of pride.

BENEFITS FOR OTHER MEMBERS OF THE COMMUNITY

- Interact with young people in positive, constructive ways, helping to overcome the misperceptions and mistrust that often exist between generations.
- Understand how young people in their community view the world, their community and themselves.
- Identify ways in which the quality of life for local young people can be improved.
- Build a stronger sense of community and pride of place.
- Appreciate the ideas and contributions of young people.
- Invest time and energy in the future of the community.

BENEFITS FOR PLANNERS AND POLICY-MAKERS

- More fully understand the needs and issues of the communities they serve.
- Make better, more informed planning and development decisions.
- Educate community members on the inherent complexities and trade-offs involved in policy and development decision-making.
- Implement at the local level the directives and spirit of the UN Convention on the Rights of the Child.
- Involve young people in efforts to implement sustainable development, thereby helping to achieve the goals of Agenda 21 and the Habitat Agenda.
- Create urban environments that are more child-friendly and humane.

© DAVID DRISKELL

The Emerging Global Policy Framework: A Call for Participation and Action

Community-based, participatory approaches to development are not new. In their modern form, they have been applied in various contexts and for various purposes since as early as the 1930s, and enjoyed fairly widespread popularity and application in the 1960s and 1970s, particularly among groups working with the poor and oppressed in Latin America, Africa and Asia.

However, the past decade has seen the emergence of a new consensus among international funding and development agencies in support of participatory approaches to development and 'child-centred development'. These agencies have turned to participatory practices as much for the practical reasons of being more effective as for the ideological reasons of supporting democratic development.[3]

Contributing to — and at times growing out of — this new international consensus on participatory development have been several key international policy documents establishing children's right to a healthy and safe environment while emphasizing the importance and value of involving young people in the decisions that affect them.

United Nations Convention on the Rights of the Child
The Convention on the Rights of the Child, adopted by the United Nations General Assembly in November 1989, is the most important international document related to children, and the first international legal instrument that establishes guarantees for the spectrum of human rights for children. States that ratify the Convention are legally accountable for their actions towards children, in accordance with the articles it sets forth.[4]

The fifty-four Articles of the Convention serve as a 'Bill of Rights' for young people, calling on the countries that ratify it to create the conditions in which children may take an active and creative part in the social and political life of their countries. It establishes children's basic right to a healthy and safe environment, as well as their right to be actors in their own development: to express their views on all matters affecting their lives; to seek, receive and impart information and ideas; and to peacefully assemble.

These and the other rights established in the Convention provide an important and valuable foundation for participatory efforts aimed at creating physical environments that respond to the needs of young people.

Related International Initiatives
Since adoption of the Convention on the Rights of the Child, a number of important initiatives have been launched that further define the framework for addressing children's rights, including:

- *Earth Summit and Agenda 21.* When world leaders gathered at the Earth Summit in Rio de Janeiro in 1992 and developed the Agenda 21 Programme of Action, they emphasized the importance of young people's participation. Children and youth were identified as major groups who must be involved in the processes of sustainable development and environmental improvement, to ensure that their interests are taken fully into account (Section 25).

- *City Summit: Children's Rights and Habitat.* Of particular importance to community development and the physical environment, the Habitat II 'City Summit' in Istanbul (1996) emphasized the need for governments to involve young people in participatory processes that shape their cities, towns and neighbourhoods.

- *Mayors, Defenders of Children.* Launched by UNICEF in 1992, this international initiative has encouraged mayors and municipal leaders to make children's basic needs a priority and increase the participation of children and other groups in community development and decision-making.

These and other international initiatives are creating a global framework for young people's participation in development efforts. This emerging framework is part of a broader effort to facilitate community-based decision-making as an essential component in the fight against poverty and the movement towards more sustainable, stable societies.

Changing Attitudes about Young People's Participation

Adults run the world. They hold the power to determine what changes should happen, when they should happen, and where they should happen.

A meaningful programme of child and youth participation requires a network of adults who have the power to implement change in the local area, are willing to engage young people in reaching consensus on what needs to be done, and are committed to using their power (ideally, assisted by young people) to make it happen. While this still provides no guarantee of success (many outside factors and constraints can affect the project outcomes), a participatory process will bear little fruit without it.

Many adults — including some who see themselves as advocates for young people — have attitudes towards young people that undermine their support for child and youth participation in community development. For example, they may see childhood as a sacred time when children should be protected from the worries and responsibilities of the adult world. Or they view young people's participation as a 'feel-good' exercise with little practical value, preferring to focus their staff and financial resources towards 'more productive ends'. Most often, young people are viewed as being unable to participate because they lack the necessary knowledge, experience and skills.

Changing adult attitudes to young people's participation is an essential step towards building the types of political support that are necessary for eventual programme success. Figure 1 provides an overview of common attitudinal barriers. The list of barriers — and responses — was developed by a group of municipal officials, planners, and youth advocates at an international workshop in 1998.

© HANNE WILHJELM

FIGURE 1

Why young people's participation is opposed, and why it should not be.[5]

Why participation is opposed	Why it should not be
Adults are here to take care of children. We should not expect children to shoulder our responsibilities.	• Young people's participation should be in conjunction with adult's participation — it is not a replacement. • Adults are not giving up their responsibilities. Rather, they are taking their responsibilities more seriously — to work hard to find out what is truly in the best interest of young people in their communities.
Involving young people in a project or decision is difficult and time-consuming — a luxury we cannot afford.	• Young people's input is critical in projects that affect them — it will lead to better decisions and better projects that are more successful in responding to young people's issues. • Participation can help to build young people's self-confidence and competence. It can also raise their community and environmental awareness, and help to develop life-long commitments and civic involvement. These are not luxuries, they are necessities. • Participation promotes creativity and innovation. • Participation promotes a sense of responsibility, respect for others, and cooperative group work, helping young people to learn about democracy. • Without young people's input, resources may be wasted — spent on something that is of little real consequence in their lives. • While it might cost more up-front, it will probably save money in the long term, as it will lead to more effective, sustainable projects and programmes. • Long-term maintenance costs can be reduced, because young people will care for what they feel they own. • Young people are the best investment we can make in the future. • Working with young people can be fun and rewarding for everyone involved.
Young people are unreliable and tend to change their minds often. They are too immature and naive to make decisions.	• Methods can be used to involve children with varied skill and maturity levels. • Some young people show these limitations; but so do some adults. • Many people who work in participatory projects with children and youth are continually amazed at how mature, insightful, and creative they can be. • The same arguments were used for many years against the participation of women in development projects.
Young people cannot foresee the long-term consequences of their actions.	• Nor can many adults. • Education is an important part of any participation process. Young people need to understand the potential consequences of their recommendations and actions. • If anyone has a stake in the future, and a concern about long-term consequences, it is young people. Their voices are critical in decisions that will affect the future.

Why participation is opposed	Why it should not be
Young people have no technical background.	• Many adults who participate in projects have no technical background. • This is an opportunity to help young people acquire new skills and understanding.
Young people make mistakes.	• Adults make mistakes too. • Mistakes are part of the learning process.
Let young people enjoy their childhood — do not thrust adult worries and responsibilities on them.	• Their childhood is being spoilt by development decisions that degrade the local places that are important to them. Through their participation, they may be able to help save such places. • Many young people are expected to earn money and take on adult responsibilities. They should also be given the right to have their say in the decisions that affect them. • The transition from childhood to adulthood does not happen overnight. Through participation, young people begin to prepare themselves for being adults. • Participation is voluntary, and does not require a great deal of young people's time. • If some young people are reluctant to participate, let them make that choice. Do not make it for them. • Participation can be fun. Young people enjoy the fact that someone is willing to listen to them.
'I was young once, so I know what children want.' Adult experts have the information and knowledge to make the best decisions in the interest of young people.	• Things have changed since adults were young. Nobody knows better than today's children and youth what it is like to be young today. • Young people themselves are the most knowledgeable on their own lives. • Outside 'experts' should facilitate, not dominate, democracy.

Making Young People's Participation Real

Making young people's participation real requires support from adults who have the power to implement change and are genuinely committed to engaging young people in the process of change.

However, even with this foundation in place, genuine participation can remain elusive. Too often, projects that claim to promote young people's participation are, on closer inspection, adult-controlled projects with little or no real participation from the young. These projects may be initiated and carried out by well-meaning adults, but the reality is that young people are told what to do or manipulated into acting in support of adult-defined initiatives.

Figure 2 illustrates a conceptual framework for thinking about young people's participation in community development, based on two primary dimensions: first, young people's power to make decisions and affect change; second, young people's interaction and collaboration with other people in the community.

FIGURE 2   The dimensions of young people's participation[6]

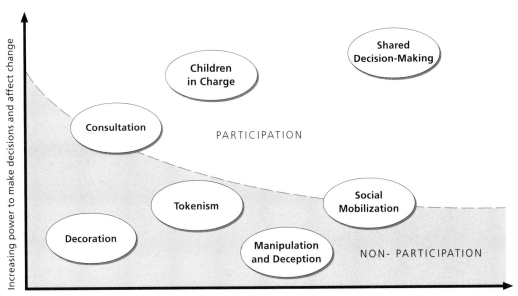

While the power to make decisions and affect change is the most important dimension (participation cannot be 'real' without some degree of power-sharing), the level of interaction and collaboration with other people in the community is also important. Real participation provides both power and interaction.

FORMS OF YOUNG PEOPLE'S PARTICIPATION

Based on the two dimensions illustrated in Figure 2, the realms of 'participation' and 'non-participation' can be defined, and various forms of interaction between young people and adults can be understood. A brief overview of these forms is provided below. For a more thorough discussion, see Chapter 3 of *Children's Participation* by Roger Hart (publication information is provided in Appendix B).

Forms of Non-participation

- **Manipulation and deception** happen when adults consciously use children to achieve their own ends without informing them about what they are doing or why. In manipulation, children often go through the motions of participation, with a seemingly high level of interaction and collaboration, while in reality they have little or no decision-making power (or even an opportunity to express their opinions in a meaningful way). Deception is when adults make claims about children's participation when in reality there was little or no actual participation.

- **Decoration** is when children are used to promote a cause even though they may have little or no idea of what they are doing or why. Little — if any — collaboration takes place and virtually no sharing of decision-making power. An example of 'decorative participation' is when children are brought on to a stage to stand behind a speaker, presumably lending credence to the speaker although unaware of why they are there or what the speech is about.

- **Tokenism** is when children appear to be participating but in fact have little or no choice about the subject or process of their participation. There may be a relatively high level of interaction, and the appearance of decision-making power, but in reality there is none at a meaningful level. An example of tokenism is when a student is selected by adults to sit on a panel and then given the mantle of representing 'the voice of youth' even though he or she has not been selected by his or her peers or has not consulted with them.

Forms of Participation

- **Consultation** is when adult decision-makers ask young people for their ideas and perspectives, and give their opinions serious consideration in making decisions. It can be a meaningful form of participation. However, depending on how it is carried out, it can also slip into the realm of non-participation, with young people given the sense of having 'had their say,' without any serious consideration given to their ideas and input. Most often, consultation does not rely on a high level of interaction or collaboration, and young people are not given a direct role in making decisions. Nevertheless, they understand why they are being asked to participate, have the option of not participating, and are informed about the results. An example of consultation is when young people are asked to give their opinions about their city as part of a survey.

- **Social mobilization** is when young people are involved in carrying out a programme or action that is initially determined by adults. Often, social mobilization slips into the realm of non-participation because young people are not informed about what they are doing and why, and are given little or no opportunity to affect the project's process or outcomes. Social mobilization typically involves higher levels of interaction than does consultation, but may provide fewer opportunities to affect decision-making. However, social mobilization *can* support meaningful participation if young people are adequately informed, their participation is voluntary, and their ideas and opinions are reflected in project decisions and outcomes. An example of social mobilization is when young people are involved in community education campaigns.

- **Children in charge** is when young people initiate an activity, make decisions, and determine outcomes. The level of interaction with other groups in the community is relatively low, but decision-making power is high (although the ability to affect change may be limited without support or assistance from well-connected adults). These can be powerful experiences for young people in terms of democratic decision-making and working with their peers to affect change in their lives. An example is a child-made clubhouse in an empty plot.

- **Shared decision-making** is when every member of the community, regardless of age or background, has the opportunity to be involved in the process and has an equal say in decision-making. Whether initiated by children or adults, the group that initiated the project realizes the value of collaboration and seeks the participation of other community members throughout the planning and decision-making process. Adults are sensitive to their role and position in the process, are attentive to the views, opinions and insights of children and youth participants, and work to ensure that adults do not dominate the group discussion or manipulate it towards their own ends. These projects are the essential building blocks for creating more vibrant democracies and communities that respond to the needs of all residents.

WHICH FORM OF PARTICIPATION IS BEST?

Shared decision-making is the ultimate goal of participatory community development, with young people treated as valued partners — maximizing their power to make decisions and affect change; as well as their interaction and collaboration with other people in the community. However, there will be times when other forms of participation are more relevant or valuable. In fact, most projects will exemplify different forms of participation at different points in the process, or even within a single project activity or event (as in the following case study). The form of participation that is most appropriate at any point in time will be based on the specific circumstances of the project. However, in all circumstances, every effort should be made to ensure that the process remains in the realm of 'participation' (as illustrated in Figure 2), reflecting the principles outlined on pages 32 to 34.

Multiple Levels of Participation in a South African Workshop

CASE STUDY

Giving Children a Voice: the Mayor's Workshop in Johannesburg, South Africa[7]
The following story from the South African site of Growing Up in Cities (GUIC) illustrates how multiple levels of participation can come into play in the course of a single event. In this example, children's participation took the forms of social mobilization, consultation, children in charge, and shared decion-making.

An Adult-Initiated Activity, with Children Invited to Participate
Over the course of several months, children from the Canaansland squatter community in Burghersdorp, Johannesburg, participated in GUIC project activities that involved them in looking at and evaluating their local area and documenting their concerns and hopes for its future.

As the culmination of the initial evaluation effort, the children were invited to speak at a municipal workshop hosted by the Mayor of Greater Johannesburg. The workshop was initiated by adult members of the project team and organized in conjunction with the Mayor's office. It provided a forum in which children from Canaansland could articulate their views directly to those with the power to help them to change the quality of their lives and to serve as a catalyst for more enlightened policies for squatter communities throughout the city. The invitees included local mayors and councillors, urban planners, and representatives of NGOs and other institutions concerned with children, as well as the children themselves and adult representatives from Canaansland.

All participants in the Mayor's Workshop were sent formal invitations, including the children of the community who had been participating in GUIC activities. The children were also invited to attend a working session to discuss their attendance and presentation before the workshop.

Children Make Decisions About their Presentation, Adults Help
At this working session, adult facilitators helped the children to define their participation in the Mayor's Workshop. The children first identified the characteristics that young participants should have. They then decided that those among them who were to meet the mayor should:

- behave well
- be clever
- be someone who knows what to do there
- be good looking
- be someone who speaks fluently
- be honest and tell the truth
- speak well

Following a suggestion from an adult researcher, the children decided that, on these grounds, all of them should participate in the workshop. Then, following a discussion about the meaning and responsibilities of democracy, they selected (by nomination and vote) two boys and two girls to speak on behalf of all of them at the workshop.

The adult project leaders worked with the four young people to help them to prepare for their presentations. Realizing that this could be a very intimidating event, the project leaders took the children to visit the municipal buildings where the workshop would be held — a place where none of them had ever been. The project leaders also made themselves available to help the children to prepare for the presentation, understanding how strongly they wanted to communicate effectively and make a good impression.

A young person from Canaansland speaks at the Mayor's workshop.

A Joint Effort: Children and Adults Speak to the Decision-Makers

Adult members of the Canaansland community were also involved in the workshop activities. The parents of the child participants were notified about their children's participation and invited to attend the workshop. A separate meeting was also held with Canaansland adults to discuss the Mayor's Workshop, identify what they felt would be important to improve the lives of their children, and select four representatives (two women and two men) to present the adults' perspectives.

Children Speak for Themselves

At the workshop, both adults and children were active participants. Most important, the children presented, in their own words, their perspectives on their lives and the place where they lived.* Their drawings of Canaansland (developed during the project) were displayed for the workshop attendees. Also, having prepared for the event, the child presenters were able to speak directly to the elected and appointed decision-makers, and let their voices be heard. They were not relegated to standing in the background while an adult spoke on their behalf. They were active, aware, and vocal participants in an event that was focused on their lives and needs. What started as an adult-initiated activity became a vehicle for various forms of child participation, giving the young people of Canaansland great pride and a sense of accomplishment.

Everyone Works Together for Change

As part of the workshop, small groups of young people and adults developed action plans for implementing improvements in Canaansland and other squatter settlements, and responding to young people's inputs and ideas. The action plan for Canaansland identified (a) goals that the community could achieve for itself; (b) goals that required external resources; and (c) goals that were the obligation of the government.

* *The children's presentation at the Mayor's workshop can be viewed on a video produced by the South African Growing Up in Cities team. See the listing for 'Growing Up in Cities: partners in research and planning', in Appendix B, for further information.*

ENDNOTES

1 Quoted in Rajni Bakshi. *Bapu Kuti: Journeys in Rediscovery of Gandhi*, New Delhi, Penguin Books, 1998.

2 Roger Hart, *Children's Participation: From Tokenism to Citizenship,* Florence, International Child Development Centre, 1992.

3 Gujit, Irene et al., editors and Victoria Johnson, guest editor. 1996. *PLA Notes, Notes on Participatory Learning and Action, Number 25. Special Issue on Children's Participation.* London: International Institute for Environment and Development, Sustainable Agriculture Programme.

4 The Convention on the Rights of the Child entered into force on 2 September 1990. As of January 2002, all Member States of the United Nations, with the exception of the USA and Somalia, had ratified the Convention. The text of the Convention can be accessed online at a number of websites, including *www.unicef.org./crc/* or *www. unhchr.org*. The text is available by post from UNICEF UK, Africa House, 64–78 Kingsway, London WC2B 6NB, UK.

5 Based on a list developed by an international group of municipal officials, planners and youth advocates who met in the Netherlands in July 1998 to explore opportunities for promoting youth participation in their respective cities (Kigali, Rwanda; Göteborg, Sweden; Rajshahi, Bangladesh; Tehran, Islamic Republic of Iran; Rotterdam, Netherlands; and Brasilia, Brazil).

6 Based on the 'Ladder of Children's Participation', in Roger Hart, *Children's Participation: The Theory and Practice of Involving Young Citizens in Community Development and Environmental Care,* pp. 40–5, New York/London, UNICEF/ Earthscan, 1997; and 'The Strategy for Interactive Decision Making', in Daniel Iacofano, *Public Involvement as an Organizational Process: A Pro-active Theory for Environmental Planning Program Management,* pp. 34–6, New York/ London, Garland Publishing, 1990.

7 Adapted from Jill Swart-Kruger (editor), *Growing Up in Canaansland: Children's Recommendations on Improving a Squatter Camp Environment,* chapter 11, Human Sciences Research Council and UNESCO-MOST Programme, 2000.

Organizing a Project

3

Young people in Oakland, California, USA, build a model to show their ideas for improving their local environment.

© ILARIA SALVADORI

Start with what they know. Build with what they have.

LAO TZU, 700 B.C.[1]

One of the most common reflections at the end of participatory projects is that not enough time was spent thinking through and preparing for the process before it began. As a result, critical information was overlooked, important groups or individuals were left out, and major obstacles or opportunities were unforeseen.

Chapters 3 to 5 are intended to help organizers avoid this major problem. This chapter outlines the organizational framework and initial activities needed as a foundation for a participatory project. Additional activities may be necessary based on the specific needs of the young people you are working with, your organization, or other factors. Chapter 4 provides ideas on how to design a sequence of activities within a cohesive participation process, while Chapter 5 reviews some of the start-up activities needed to get the project under way.

Project Checklist

The following checklist will help you to think through some of the issues that need to be considered as you start your project. Because these issues can be complex, the initial project-planning activities should involve individuals who have special insights into the local community and the issues that affect it. This is one of the key values behind establishing a Project Coordinating Team (see page 51).

Review the questions in each section of the checklist. If you cannot answer 'yes' to any of the questions, refer to the appropriate section later in this chapter for more information. As you go through the checklist, consider whether additional questions need to be added for your specific project.

Project Coordinating Team (page 51)

❑ *Does your organization already have a working group that can serve as a Project Coordinating Team?*

❑ *Does that group include representatives from all the groups who will be interested in and potentially affected by the project, including children and youth from the local area?*

❑ *Is the group of a workable size (less than ten) to effectively oversee the project start-up activities?*

Goals, Opportunities and Constraints (page 52)

❑ *Is there a clear and common understanding of pre-defined goals and expected outcomes for the project based on:*
   (1) the mission of your organization?
   (2) the requirements of funding agencies?
   (3) the personal goals and desires of key team members?

❏ *Do the pre-defined goals for the project leave enough opportunity for child and youth participants to have a meaningful say in determining the project's direction and outcomes?*

❏ *Is there an appreciation within your group or organization about participation as a worthwhile goal in and of itself?*

❏ *Have the project's pre-defined goals and expected outcomes been communicated clearly to all participants?*

❏ *Has your group or organization evaluated existing opportunities for the project that might contribute to its overall success and effectiveness?*

❏ *Is there a common understanding about the potential barriers and constraints on the project?*

Site Selection (page 55)

❏ *Have the general parameters for selecting a site been defined (i.e. identification of a specific socio-economic group or type of settlement that will be the focus of the project work)?*

❏ *Has the selection been made of the specific site (or sites) in which the project will take place?*

❏ *Is the site appropriate for the resources that are available and the goals that have been defined?*

❏ *If the project site is large, has thought been given to doing a 'pilot project' on a relatively small scale in a well-defined area as a means of developing staff capacities and creating a positive local example of the benefits of child and youth participation?*

Child and Youth Participants (page 56)

❏ *Has the size and composition of the participant group been defined, considering all the relevant factors:*
  - *age*
  - *group size*
  - *gender*
  - *economic status*
  - *race, ethnicity, language, and religion*
  - *availability*

❏ *Have strategies been identified for making contact with potential child and youth participants and encouraging their participation?*

❏ *Do child and youth participants represent 'invisible' members of the community (i.e. the most disenfranchised community members who are rarely reached by development projects, such as children with special needs)? If not, is there a workable strategy for encouraging and facilitating their participation?*

Stakeholder Assessment (page 60)

❏ *Have the project's adult and institutional stakeholders (i.e. groups and individuals, other than children and youth, who will be interested in or potentially affected by the project) been identified, including those people and organizations whose support will be needed to implement the project and its recommendations?*

❏ *Have the interests, motivations, and perspectives of each stakeholder been considered?*

❏ *Is there a workable strategy for contacting all the stakeholders, involving them in the process, and keeping them informed about project developments?*

❏ *Has the role of the local media in relation to the project been considered?*

❏ *Are the key project stakeholders represented on the Project Coordinating Team?*

Staffing (page 61)

❏ *Have staffing resources been defined, taking into consideration the ability and willingness of staff to participate in a project such as this?*

❏ *Has there been an open and honest discussion about the roles that staff members would like to serve in the project and the level of commitment that they are able and willing to give to it?*

❏ *Have strategies for supplementing staff resources been considered, such as hiring new staff, partnering with another organization, bringing in local professionals, or finding outside volunteers?*

Scheduling (page 62)

❏ *Have realistic time commitments been defined for each team member, as well as the level of time commitment that can be expected from volunteers, child and youth participants and other stakeholders?*

❏ *Have other scheduling constraints been considered?*

❏ *Has enough time been allocated to project start-up activities and a realistic project start date identified?*

❏ *Has a rough project timeline been developed?*

Funding (page 63)

❏ *Has a realistic budget been developed, including staffing, materials, equipment, office space, outside services and other project needs?*

❏ *Are there adequate financial resources to support project activities?*

❏ *If not, have potential sources of external funding been identified, and adequate time allowed for project fund-raising?*

❏ *Are potential funding agencies willing to invest in a participatory process in which the participants will have a say in determining the project's outcomes?*

❏ *Are there workable strategies for reducing project costs or increasing the project's attractiveness to potential funding agencies (in-kind donations, implementing the project in phases, etc.)?*

Project Coordinating Team

ROLES

The Project Coordinating Team oversees the start-up activities and establishes a participatory framework for the project. The group will help to develop strategies, solve problems and provide general guidance for the project. The members can also help to build a network of supporters and serve as liaisons to potential funders, local government agencies, youth groups and other individuals or organizations who may have an interest in the project. Although much of their time will be committed towards the beginning of the project, they can remain active throughout the whole project, helping to respond to issues as they arise and maintaining constructive relationships with key individuals and organizations.

COMPOSITION

The composition of the Project Coordinating Team will depend on an initial assessment of the key stakeholders. 'Stakeholders' are the people and organizations that will be affected by or interested in your project (see page 60).

Every Project Coordinating Team should include:
- **Child and youth representatives** from the community you will be working in;
- **Adult representatives from the community** (local leaders or elders, parents, teachers, etc.);
- **Field staff** who will be involved in carrying out the project.

Other groups to consider for inclusion on the Project Coordinating Team are:

- **Local government representatives** (municipal planning staff, local councillors, youth advocates, etc.);
- **Volunteers and local resource people** (those with skills or knowledge that will be useful in the project, such as design and planning professionals, researchers, photographers, journalists, health professionals, local college students, etc.);
- **Other people in your organization** (director, fund-raiser, trainer, etc.);
- **People from other organizations** (representatives from child and youth advocacy organizations, local development or youth-serving agencies, local business community, local trade unions, etc.);
- **Funding agency representatives** (those who have given, or may possibly give, financial resources to support the project).

The participation of community stakeholders — including child and youth representatives — can help tap into community resources and establish an ongoing network of support to facilitate implementation of the project's outcomes.

CHILD AND YOUTH REPRESENTATIVES

To maximize the participation of young people in the project, child and youth representatives should be involved in the project-planning process. They are the most familiar with the issues facing young people in the community, and will have good ideas on how to make contact with young people in the area and generate interest in the project. They will also bring a fresh perspective to the planning process, and provide a foundation for child and youth control and ownership of the project's subsequent activities.

Child or youth representatives can be selected in any number of ways. For example, selection can be based on young people's previous interactions through your organization's programmes or their position as representatives in other organizations (e.g. student council members or leaders of a local youth group).

As members of the Project Coordinating Team, they should participate as equals with adults in the team's proceedings. Their roles and responsibilities should be clearly communicated before they agree to take part, and they should be actively encouraged to voice their opinions and take part fully in the project-planning effort.

SIZE

As a working group, the Project Coordinating Team should be kept to a manageable size (less than ten). However, you may find it politically necessary or beneficial to involve more people. In that case, consider having a larger team and having them select a smaller 'Steering Committee' from their ranks to provide more hands-on involvement based on the overall direction established by the whole team.

Goals, Opportunities and Constraints

PRE-DEFINED GOALS AND EXPECTED OUTCOMES

Most projects begin with a set of pre-defined goals and expected outcomes that establish clear parameters for the project before most of the participants even know that the project exists. These need to be clearly identified in the project start-up phase.

- **Identify pre-defined goals and expected outcomes.** As part of the project start-up activities, consider the goals that may already have been defined for the project based on the mission of your organization, your own reasons for undertaking the project, and the requirements of funding agencies. These pre-defined goals and expected outcomes establish basic project parameters within which a programme of activities can be developed. Questions to consider include:

  > What do you and other adult participants or sponsors hope will happen as a result of the project?

© NILDA COSCO

Members of the eight Growing Up in Cities teams (see page 19) met together to establish common goals, agree on a common project approach and core methodology, and facilitate communication between the different site teams.

> Are there measurable, identifiable outcomes that you, the funding agency or others would like to see achieved?

> Who will benefit from the project? In what ways will the community benefit? How will the project's participants benefit?

> How much real control will the community and/or young people have over determining project goals and outcomes?

> To what extent is a participatory approach feasible and achievable in this context?

> Can some of the pre-defined goals or expected outcomes be modified so that local participants will have a greater voice in establishing the project's direction and defining its outcomes?

• **Ensure transparency.** To maintain the integrity of participation, the goals and priorities of all participants need to be clearly communicated to everyone involved, including young participants. Everyone needs to be told plainly, clearly and honestly why the project is being undertaken and what the sponsoring organization and/or funding agency hopes to achieve. Participants can then define their own goals, within those parameters, to incorporate their needs and perspectives.

• **Value participation as a goal in itself.** In defining your preliminary goals and expectations, remember that participation is a worthwhile goal in and of itself.

OPPORTUNITIES

Consider opportunities that might strengthen the project's chances of success and facilitate its implementation, such as:

• **Friends in strategic places** who might have the resources and influence to implement changes recommended by the project.

- **Renewed public interest in youth issues** due to recent events or local media coverage.
- **A community event or celebration** that could be related to the project, providing a forum for displaying young people's ideas or an opportunity for community-wide participation activities.
- **An upcoming election** in which local politicians are looking for community initiatives to showcase (care should be taken so that the project does not become a political issue or become co-opted in ways that undermine its participatory principles).
- **A friendly journalist** who could provide positive coverage in the local media and give voice to young people's issues, ideas and concerns.
- **A related community development effort,** such as redevelopment of a local commercial area or a pending development proposal, providing an opportunity for incorporating young people's perspectives in an existing project of community-wide concern.

BARRIERS AND CONSTRAINTS

What are the potential barriers and constraints that might hinder or block the project's implementation or compromise its potential for success? The following are examples of barriers that may need to be considered:

- **Stakeholder opposition,** because they see the project as being counter to their interests or as compromising their decision-making authority.

Unforeseen barriers and constraints can throw a project off-course, cause it to lose momentum, and limit its effectiveness. Knowing in advance what the barriers and constraints are gives you a chance to prepare for them and maneuver your project accordingly.

- **Official resistance** from elected representatives or bureaucrats who see participation as an added complication to their job and therefore something to be avoided, rather than an opportunity for constructive engagement with the community.
- **Organizational issues,** in which individuals or groups within the sponsoring organization are unfamiliar with participation or unwilling to work in participatory ways and share their decision-making authority.
- **Community apathy or cynicism** from previous 'participatory' efforts in the community that resulted in nothing or ended up serving outside interests, but not those of the community.
- **Political infighting** among local groups, in which the project could become an initiative that one group embraces and the other fights against.
- **Lack of funding** to support the participatory process and/or implementation of its recommendations.

As potential barriers and constraints are identified, consider how to structure the project or implement countermeasures to overcome or remove them before they cause problems.

See page 38 for a list of common reasons people give for opposing young people's participation, and responses.

The Growing Up in Cities sites all focused on similar project settings of low-income, working class communities. However, the characteristics and actual physical size of the project sites varied, based on local circumstances and resources, from a single apartment complex in Oakland, California, USA (LEFT), to a working class neighborhood in Trondheim, Norway (BELOW LEFT), to a squatter settlement in Johannesburg, South Africa (BELOW).

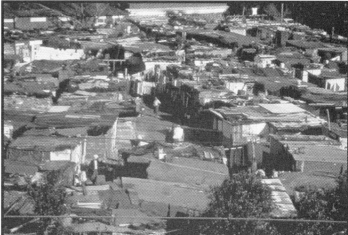

Site Selection

In some cases, the project site may already be determined. In other cases, a deliberate decision may need to be made. As a first step towards selecting a specific site, identify the general socio-economic group and type of settlement or community that will be the focus of the project (e.g. central city neighbourhood, squatter camp, street children). This is the *project setting*. It may be determined based on your organization's or group's programme focus, by the fact that you are more familiar with or have greater access to some areas or sites over others, or by current trends, policy issues or other factors that are in need of attention, investigation and action. The Project Coordinating Team should select the setting in which they feel the project will be most appropriate and effective, where engagement with young people will make the greatest difference.

Once the general setting is determined, the *project site* must be defined (i.e. the specific geographical area or areas on which to focus). Its size should be based on the resources available. Large or highly populated areas will obviously require greater commitments of time, staffing and financial resources. Because participatory projects require group interaction, it is best to select a relatively well-defined area that is manageable in size. If the area is large, one or more small pilot projects could be done as a first phase.

If you need to raise funds to cover project costs, think strategically about how your site selection will aid or hinder your ability to do so. If the Project Coordinating Team sees great need at a particular setting or site, think creatively about alternative ways to cover the project's costs. For example, you might consider approaching non-traditional funding sources (such as a local business group or charitable organization); presenting the project in a different light (e.g. presenting it as a transport improvement project or environmental education project instead of a youth participation project); or finding ways to reduce the costs of the project (e.g. through use of volunteers or an abbreviated activities schedule).

Child and Youth Participants

Children and youth are the most important project stakeholders. You will need to consider and define the following factors when identifying potential child and youth participants:

- **Age.** What age groups do you hope to involve? This will have a big impact on the scope and depth of the participatory activities you undertake. Consider the age of participants in relation to the preliminary goals and expected outcomes identified for the project. See the discussion on 'Age-appropriateness,' page 76.

- **Size of group.** How many young participants can you realistically involve, given your staffing and financial resources?

- **Gender.** Consider gender-related issues that might affect young people's participation. Are girls allowed to interact in mixed groups? Will they feel free to speak their mind in the company of boys, or is it necessary to have separate gender-based groups for some activities? Consider how these issues will impact on the project and try to create a framework in which both genders can participate to the full extent of their abilities, striving for equal representation of boys and girls.

- **Economic status.** Consider the socio-economic status of child and youth participants, and how that might affect the project's approach and design.

- **Race, ethnicity, language and religion.** Try to reflect the composition of the local community among the young people involved in your project. If there are minority groups in the community that are intimidated by the majority, consider ways of reaching out to them and ensuring their full participation.

- **Availability.** Consider young people's schedules. Are they attending school full time? Are they working? Do they have family or work obligations in the evenings or at weekends? Will they be on holiday from school in the middle of the project? A flexible project schedule will be required so that young people with other commitments can participate.

Once you have defined these parameters, you will want to consider strategies for making contact with potential participants and stimulating their interest in the project. See 'Making contact' on page 87.

Developing a 'representative sample'

In identifying potential participants, try to ensure that the participants are representative of the community that you are trying to understand. This is especially important if the results of your project will be used to make comparisons with other project sites or to develop generalizations about a larger population of young people. To make sure that participants are representative of the larger population, you will first need to find out as much as possible about that population. What is the breakdown in terms of gender, age, family income, caste or class, ethnic or religious group, type of schooling, work status, type of housing, and general health? Once you have a good understanding of the 'profile' of the population, you will want to assemble a group of participants who represent a similar profile. This 'representative sample' will make it possible to draw conclusions from the local project that can be inferred as being generally true of the larger population as well (even then, all generalizations should be qualified by a statement regarding the limitations of the research that was conducted).

REACHING OUT TO 'INVISIBLE GROUPS'

Be sure to seek out 'invisible' members of communities — the ones who are usually the most disenfranchised, and whom most development projects never reach. Invisible members could include children with disabilities, working children and youth, children in extreme poverty, or children and youth belonging to religious or ethnic minorities. The discussion on the following pages by Nilda Cosco specifically covers the issue of involving children with special needs in participatory processes.

These groups should be identified as significant stakeholders, with particular attention given to understanding their situations and facilitating their participation. Consider the attitudinal, cultural and practical barriers that have kept them hidden from development efforts, and define potential strategies for tailoring the participatory process and project activities to their schedule, needs and issues.

© DAVID DRISKELL

Extending the Participatory Process to Children with Special Needs BY NILDA COSCO

Children with special needs have a right to participate according to their level of ability. By special needs, we mean children who have a sensory, motor, psychological or learning disability as well as children 'at risk' — those living in impoverished environments or under difficult circumstances such as war. As any other participant, they bring to our attention, in unique ways, their preferences, needs and values. Their contributions are as valuable as those from any other member of the community.

Young people with disabilities celebrate their success in convincing the municipal government in Buenos Aires, Argentina, to install ramps to make wheelchair travel possible from their school to a neighbourhood plaza.

The inclusion of children with disabilities in the participation process appears to be easier when dealing with children and youth who have sensory impairments (deafness, blindness) or motor disabilities, but more difficult when dealing with children who have learning, mental or psychological impairments. Facilitators should be aware that all children, including those with multiple disabilities, can contribute to the process if they are appropriately guided.

The Convention on the Rights of the Child supports the participation of children and recognizes their evolving capacity to participate. Article 23 of the Convention further supports the right of a child with physical or mental disabilities to 'enjoy a full and decent life, in conditions which ensure dignity, promote self-reliance, and facilitate the child's active participation in the community'. Parents and other adults have a responsibility to facilitate the participation of all children, regardless of disability, in a manner consistent with the child's age and maturity, creating the right atmosphere to allow each child to freely express his or her views. The participation of young people with disabilities — like the participation of any young person — implies the understanding that they are valuable members of the community who have something to contribute to society.

Children with disabilities living in low-income communities face additional difficulties in the daily struggle for survival. Health programmes are scarce for everybody and extremely meagre for children who need long-term care. Severe cases are institutionalized, as families cannot afford treatments and daily care. Others remain at home, visiting the hospital or local health-care units several times a week, often a long and complicated procedure since most low-income families rely on public transport. Family routines, in these cases, are severely disrupted. Some children do not even have access to special care.

Local cultures have different assumptions about the meaning of being disabled and a child with disabilities can become a stigma for the family. This is one of the reasons why the participation of these children is important. It is a way for them to become visible, to be part of the community of children. Visibility communicates a strong message of inclusion and it also helps to promote their inclusion at the family level. Parents and siblings learn to value the contributions from the child with disabilities when they see how the rest of the group regards his or her opinions.

In planning sessions to include children with disabilities, consider the following:

- Make contact with social workers, therapists and community organizations such as churches to identify prospective children with special needs.
- Send out a message of universal acceptance. Make clear that *all* abilities are welcome.
- Ask families or community groups to let you know in advance if children with special needs will be attending your programme. This will help facilitators to be adequately prepared.
- Consult with experts in different disabilities to prepare adequate materials and tailored questions to get the most from participants.
- Sign-language interpreters and cards with graphic instructions may be helpful. Black on white or yellow printed matter helps readability.
- The use of simple language, or other artefacts to assist communication, is recommended, as well as processes such as structured role-playing and games.
- During meetings, sit at the same level as the children in order to make good eye contact.
- Open meetings by welcoming the participants, introducing them by name, and present the steps that you are going to follow. Make sure that the children with disabilities have properly understood the process.
- Allow interaction of siblings as helpers/interpreters. Ask them what is the best way to communicate with the child if you are insecure.
- Provide a calm atmosphere, without background noise.
- Concentrate your questions on two or three main issues.
- Remember that instructions and questions must be simple and direct.
- Allow enough time to respond to questions. Do not repeat a question until the child has shown that he or she has not understood.
- Do not hesitate to ask the child to repeat their answer to aid clarity of expression.
- If a child has a hearing impairment, be sure there is no background noise, that the child is able to see the faces of other participants, and pay attention to gestures and signs that the child may make.
- Children with physical disabilities may feel tired quickly. Be open to signs of tiredness and be ready to give a break or to reschedule the session.
- For a child with visual impairments, prepare the room without obstacles and conduct the meeting in a well-illuminated area. Avoid glare. Do not hesitate to use the words 'look' or 'see'.
- Always allow enough time to establish rapport. This is especially important for children at risk or living under difficult circumstances because they need to build trust in the facilitators in order to open up and express themselves.

Stakeholder Assessment

A 'stakeholder assessment' is the process of thinking carefully and strategically about who will be affected by or interested in a project (in addition to children and youth). This may include individuals, groups or organizations in one or more of the following four categories.

- **The community.** This is the largest and most critical stakeholder group. It includes all members of the community who want to participate or will be affected by the project, regardless of age, gender, race, language, religion or economic status. Examples of community stakeholders include children and youth, parents, residents and business owners.

- **Organizations and institutions.** These may be groups or organizations that are active in the local community, but which also extend outside the local community. Examples include local government departments, schools and universities, business and service organizations, religious groups and institutions, NGOs, youth advocacy groups, professional associations and international aid or development agencies. They can be critical players in the process itself as well as in the implementation of the ideas that the project generates.

- **Outside professionals.** These are the professional 'experts' who bring specialized skills or knowledge pertinent to the project and community. They might include planners, architects, researchers, sociologists, engineers or educators, among others. Their expertise is often critical to the success of the project, although they participate with the understanding that they are there to collaborate with the community and assist the community's process — not to make decisions on behalf of the community or to promote their own agenda.

- **Process managers.** These are the individuals who help to manage and facilitate the participatory process. They organize meetings and activities, mediate between different points of view, help to ensure that technical information is made accessible to everyone, and ensure that all participants are involved in a meaningful way. They help the group to respond to crises as they occur and keep the project moving forward.

Questions to ask when conducting a stakeholder assessment include:
> Who will be impacted or affected by the project?
> Whose support or involvement will be critical to the project's success?
> Are there key individuals or groups who must be 'won over'?
> What are the interests, motivations and perspectives of each individual or group?
> Are the individuals or groups organized? Do they speak with one voice?
> What can they bring to (or take away from) the project?
> How will the project contact and involve them?
> What role might the local media play in relation to the project?

A successful stakeholder assessment will identify not only who should be involved, but also whose support will be critical for implementation of ideas that may emerge from the project.

Support can come from the most unexpected places. Avoid making broad generalizations or relying on stereotypes to determine whether or not a certain person or group is going to support the project. Try to put yourself in the other's shoes, and think about how they would perceive and respond to the type of initiative you are undertaking. Present the project to them in terms that they will respond to and support.

Some form of initial stakeholder assessment will be needed to identify candidates for the Project Coordinating Team. Once the team is in place, its members can help to identify other stakeholders in the community, answering the questions listed above. A preliminary stakeholder assessment may also help in determining the desirability of one project site over another.

A thorough assessment of project stakeholders at the very beginning of the project can help establish the foundation for a successful project.

As the project moves forward, make sure that key stakeholders are involved in the process or kept informed about the project's developments. Think about ways to constructively engage them, tapping into community resources in the process. Local planners, architects, teachers and other professionals may find it personally gratifying to be involved in a project working with young people. They will appreciate the fact that you thought of them and made the effort to include them.

Also, be careful to consider the past experiences — positive and negative — that groups or individuals may have had in the community. The involvement of groups or individuals with poor reputations in the local area can potentially undermine the project's credibility.

Throughout the project, it is vital to keep in mind the following question when evaluating progress: Who is not participating, and why?

Logistics: Staffing, Scheduling and Funding

STAFFING

Consider your available staffing resources and the ability and willingness of your staff to participate in a project such as the one you are planning. Some staff will find a participatory project to be very stimulating and will gladly accept the challenge; others may find it to be too overwhelming and taxing.

Involve key staff members in your review of available resources, and have an open and honest discussion about the roles that each would like to play in the project (see 'Organizing and Training Project Staff', page 80). Remember that not everyone is comfortable or even appropriate in each of these roles. Work with staff members to define the role or roles in which they would like to serve, and the level of commitment that they are able and willing to give to the project.

If staff resources are inadequate either in terms of availability or skills, consider strategies for enhancing those resources, such as:

> Hiring new staff.

> Teaming up with staff from another local organization, which will require addressing issues of organizational culture, coordination, time and resource allocation, and clear definition of roles and responsibilities.

> Bringing in local professionals who may have relevant skills (architects, engineers, planners, educators, artists, researchers, etc.) and who may find the project to be a personally rewarding experience. Contact local professional organizations, service clubs or universities to locate potential resource persons.

> Finding outside volunteers to assist in the project, such as students from a local university, older youth or community residents who live in or near the project site, or retired people who might be interested in working with local young people.

SCHEDULING

Project scheduling should take into consideration the time constraints that young people face, whether they work or are in school.

Time is a valuable resource, as are staffing and funding. It also plays an important role in defining the logistical parameters and limitations of projects.

Consider the level of time commitment that team members can realistically make to the project, given their other commitments. Also, consider the level of time commitment that can be expected from volunteers, child and youth participants, and other members of the community. This will provide you with a rough estimate of how many hours of project activities can realistically take place in a typical day, week or month.

Also identify any time and schedule constraints that will affect the project. For example, does the project need to correspond to organizational budget cycles? Do young people only have time available at certain hours of the day or week? Will they be in school, on holiday or taking exams during the course of the project? Are there seasonal issues to be considered such as monsoon rains, harvest time or winter?

© S.R. PRAKASH

With these time-related issues in mind, develop a rough timeline for the project. Start by making a conservative estimate of how long it will take to organize the necessary resources for carrying out the project and set a realistic 'project start date'. Once the start date is determined, identify key dates for achieving the main project activities. Be sure to allocate enough time for conducting the participatory activities, doing the necessary analysis, making group decisions and engaging in critical reflection with the participants.

This rough project timeline can be used as the basis for developing a more detailed process design, as described in Chapter 4, as well as for developing a clearer understanding of project staffing and funding needs.

FUNDING

Some organizations will have adequate financial resources to support project activities, while others will need to locate external funding support.

Finding external funding for participatory development projects can be problematic and time-consuming due to the inherent contradictions between many funding agency requirements and the nature of participatory planning. Most funding agencies want to have measurable outcomes that can be defined at the start and quantified at the end. They want to know what programme will be launched, what will be built, what will be published, and how many people will benefit. Defining such outcomes can be difficult or impossible in projects where the process is as important as the product, and where decision-making about project outcomes is vested in the local community. Specific, defined outcomes will only be determined after the project has begun, when participants have delved into the local issues and developed an action plan.

After having difficulty in finding financial support for a 'research project' with young people, the Growing Up in Cities site in India recast the project as a 'data collection' effort as part of a larger community planning project, which then attracted funders' interest.

Potential funding sources might include government departments, charitable foundations, philanthropic agencies, international aid agencies, corporations or the local community itself. Think creatively about potential funding sources for your project, and allocate plenty of time in the project start-up phase for seeking and securing funding support. Developing a Project Start-up Plan (page 78) can provide an effective fund-raising tool. It helps to communicate the project's structure and purpose to potential funding agencies, and demonstrates the level of commitment and thought behind the funding proposal.

Professionals and communities seeking funds for participatory projects should consider the following:

> How much money will be needed, roughly, to cover staffing, materials, equipment, office space, outside services and other project needs?

> How much money will be available within the organization or community for carrying out this project? Will the local government provide financial resources or other forms of support?

> Will the definition of the project affect the resources that are available (i.e. one type of project may attract support while another type would make it difficult to obtain funding)?

> What are the most promising external funding sources for this type of project in this area?
> Who has the authority to make decisions on resource allocation that can help this project? How can you best win their support?
> Are there opportunities to use 'in-kind' donations from local businesses (they donate the material or service in return for recognition as a supporter of the project)?
> Can the use of volunteers help to reduce project costs?
> Would use of a 'phasing' approach make the project more fundable, with the first phase including basic planning activities and the second phase devoted to implementation?

ENDNOTE

[1] Quoted in Gerard Salole, *Building on People's Strengths: The Case for Contextual Child Development,* Save the Children, Zimbabwe, 1992.

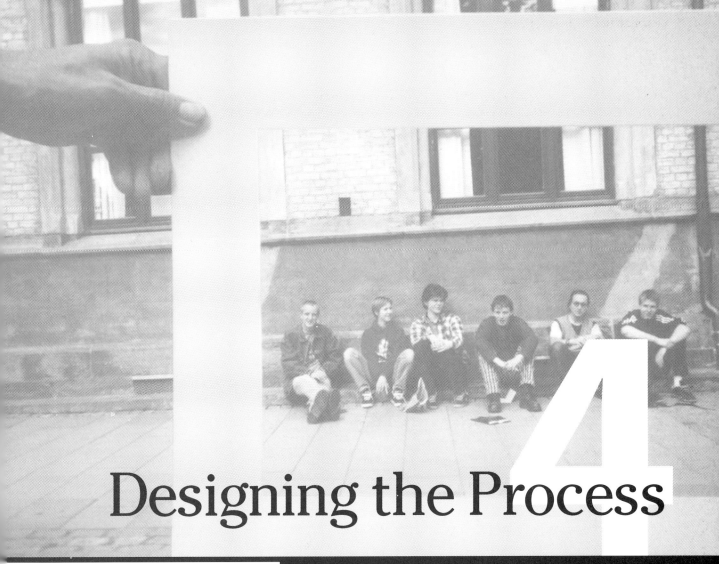

Designing the Process

Young people in Melbourne, Australia, use 'frames' in a photography exercise that explores their local environment.

© KAREN MALONE

Participation is not a political campaign that puts children first…but a process of creating a society that is inclusive of young citizens.

BRIAN MILNE[1]

A successful participation programme provides a logical sequence of activities and events to lead participants, together, from identifying and understanding a problem to solving it. It relies on careful planning and hard work, and draws upon the wisdom, insights and creativity of all participants.

While the previous chapter focused on the organizational framework and initial activities needed to get a project off the ground, this chapter focuses on the actual design of a participatory process. It provides an approach for thinking about which methods to use and how to sequence them. The methods themselves are described in detail in Chapter 6, Participation Toolkit.

The Participatory Planning Process

Figure 3 illustrates the basic components of a participatory process and the relationship between them: the project's *context,* the *stakeholders* who are involved, and the *activities* that constitute the actual process in action.

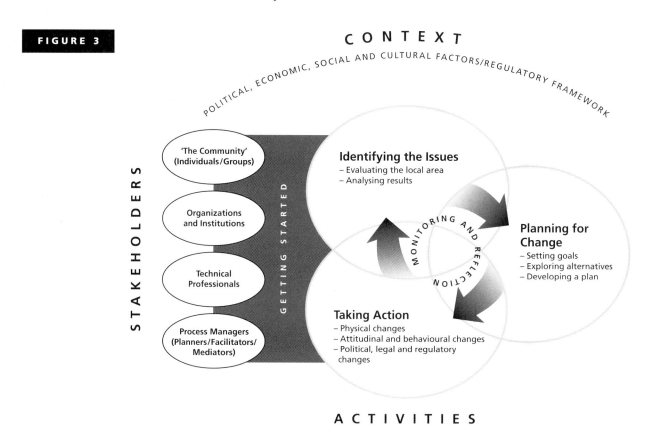

FIGURE 3

CONTEXT

POLITICAL, ECONOMIC, SOCIAL AND CULTURAL FACTORS/REGULATORY FRAMEWORK

STAKEHOLDERS

'The Community' (Individuals/Groups)

Organizations and Institutions

Technical Professionals

Process Managers (Planners/Facilitators/Mediators)

GETTING STARTED

Identifying the Issues
– Evaluating the local area
– Analysing results

MONITORING AND REFLECTION

Planning for Change
– Setting goals
– Exploring alternatives
– Developing a plan

Taking Action
– Physical changes
– Attitudinal and behavioural changes
– Political, legal and regulatory changes

ACTIVITIES

CONTEXT

As emphasized in Chapter 3, Organizing a Project, a number of issues can shape or affect a participatory planning project, including political, economic, social and cultural factors. These create potential opportunities as well as potential barriers and constraints. The local, regional or national 'regulatory framework' must also be considered — the laws, rules and regulations that may affect the project and its ability to create change. These issues are not addressed at length in this manual, but understanding and responding to them provides an essential foundation for a successful project.

STAKEHOLDERS

Participatory projects must be inclusive, as emphasized in the preceding chapters. They should involve children and youth as well as the different categories of stakeholders shown in Figure 3 (and discussed on page 60).

ACTIVITIES

The participatory planning process generally begins with 'Identifying the issues' and progresses to 'Planning for change' and 'Taking action'. However, these phases do not always progress in a neat, orderly fashion. A process that is truly participatory, reflective and responsive will reassess previous assumptions and project directions as new information, attitudes, barriers and opportunities come to light. This may cause the project to alter its course 'midstream' or to revisit previous activities.

The following is an overview of the basic phases in a participatory project.

Young people gather data on the local area, identifying issues and opportunities for further review and study.

1. **Getting started.** This includes all the tasks and activities involved in getting a project under way. As with other project activities, it may be necessary to revisit some of these initial activities as the project progresses (for example, adding a new member to the Project Coordinating Team when a previously unidentified stakeholder group emerges, or conducting ongoing training with project staff). Activities for getting started are described in Chapters 3, 4 and 5 of this manual.

2. **Identifying the issues.** Most projects actually start when someone identifies the need or desire to change a given situation. This initial inspiration can come from any number of sources, such as concerned community members, community-based organizations, parents, teachers, local government or international aid agencies. Ideally, young people themselves are the project instigators or, at a minimum, involved in assessing 'the problem' and determining a course of action.

Children at a new settlement site in Johannesburg, South Africa, work with adults on plans to transform a shipping container into a quiet study room for older children and a morning creche for younger children.

© JILL SWART-KRUGER

Two types of activity are typically involved in this phase of the participatory process:

> *Evaluating the local area.* Participants try to understand as much as possible about their situation and the factors that may influence their ability to take action. Activities might include data collection about the local area (see Appendix A) as well as participatory exercises to involve young people and other community members, organizations and institutions in the environmental evaluation process (see Chapter 6). Technical professionals may also contribute their skills and perspectives to this process, presenting their input to the community in an accessible language and format.

> *Analysing results.* Through the information-gathering and evaluation process, participants develop a stronger sense of issues and opportunities in their local area and a greater appreciation of various viewpoints in the community. They then begin to look for recurrent themes, significant patterns and hidden issues, developing a common understanding of the problem or issues on which they want to focus their efforts (see 'Analysing the results', page 162).

3. **Planning for change.** In this phase, participants develop a plan for addressing the problem or key issues. This involves setting goals, exploring alternatives and developing a plan of action. These activities are discussed in detail in Chapter 7.

> *Setting goals.* Participants agree on a set of goals in response to the identified problem or set of issues.

> *Exploring alternatives.* Participants consider alternative strategies for achieving the stated goals, taking into consideration the strengths and weaknesses of each approach, and define a set of strategies that they believe will be most effective.

> *Developing a plan.* Participants develop a strategic plan of action that outlines the process and results of their work and sets forth the strategies and sequence of actions that have been agreed upon.

4. **Taking action.** Participants and other organizations, agencies or individuals undertake a series of actions to put the plan into practice. Actions may be oriented towards making a physical change in the local area; fostering an attitudinal or behavioural change; or undertaking a political, legal or regulatory change (see 'Taking action', page 170).

5. **Monitoring and reflection.** Participatory community development is a long-term process of community action, change and renewal. Two essential components of this on-going process are (a) monitoring the plan's implementation and its achievements; and (b) reflection on the process itself, both at its conclusion and at key milestones. These activities help to ensure that the project remains relevant and effective. They also allow participants to consider the extent of their success, and to identify the barriers that kept them from being more successful. This may lead to the definition of additional projects or actions, reconsideration of the project's goals, or revision of the key strategies being employed to address community issues.[2]

Designing a Process

In designing a participatory process, it is important to think through the entire sequence of activities, from 'Getting started' to 'Monitoring and reflection'. While it is not possible or even desirable to plan out all the activities at the very beginning of the project, it is useful to consider the time and resources needed to support each phase.

Use the 'Process Design Worksheet' on the following page to think through the basic parameters of the five project phases described above.

To facilitate participation of the Project Coordinating Team, use a large sheet of paper taped to the wall or similar writing surface. Work through each phase and sequence of questions with the entire team, developing a first draft relatively quickly, and then revisiting those areas where more detail or thought is needed.

Once completed, the Process Design Worksheet will provide the basic information needed to establish the sequence of project activities and to define the level of effort and resource support needed (at least for the initial phases).

Process design worksheet

This worksheet template can help you to think through the process design for your project. For each phase, consider the questions listed in the left-hand column of the worksheet. Since it will not be possible to fit all the information you generate onto a single worksheet, consider making a separate worksheet for each phase.

	Getting Started	Identifying the Issues
What? What are the goals for this phase? What will be produced or achieved?		
Who? What groups or individuals need to be involved in this phase?		
How? What methods will be used to involve the participants in achieving the goals? Will other tasks need to be done in this phase (data collection, networking, logistics, etc.)? What staff, materials, funding and other resources will be needed?		
When? When will the phase begin and end?		

anning for Change	Taking Action	Monitoring and Reflection

Developing a Process Flow-Chart

A 'Process Flow-Chart' is a graphic representation of the sequence of project activities, showing how they relate to each other and their approximate duration. It is a useful project-planning tool, as well as an easy way to communicate the project activities and schedule.

Following are brief instructions for developing a Process Flow-Chart, similar to the example shown in Figure 4 on pages 74–75. To facilitate participation of the Project Coordinating Team in developing the diagram, use a large sheet of paper taped to the wall or similar writing surface.

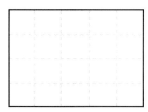

THE GRID

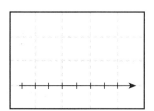

THE TIMELINE

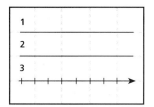

PROCESS TRACKS

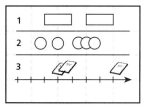

ACTIVITIES

STEP 1

Draw a grid. Draw a light grid (in pencil) of vertical and horizontal lines to provide a basic framework for the diagram.

STEP 2

Establish the timeline. Along the bottom of the grid, draw a line representing the project timeline. Indicate on the timeline the approximate start and end dates for each project phase. For an initial process diagram, it will probably be necessary to illustrate the first three phases (through 'Planning for change').

STEP 3

Define the 'process tracks'. Divide the rest of the paper horizontally into sections or 'process tracks'. These help to differentiate between different types of activity and task. For example, one process track might show team meetings, another could show participation activities, another could identify larger community events related to the project, and another could highlight key products or outcomes. The three tracks shown in Figure 4 are 'Participation activities', 'Team meetings,' and 'Products/outcomes'.

STEP 4

Illustrate the sequence of activities. Use simple visuals, icons or text boxes to illustrate the sequence of activities and outcomes in relation to the timeline (see Figure 4). Indicate where activities take place simultaneously or overlap. When working with a group, place pieces of paper marked with the various project activities (ideally in different shapes and/or colours to depict the different types of activity) on the grid based on the group's discussion. Lightly tape the pieces of paper in place so that they can be moved.

STEP 5

Show relationships. Illustrate the relationship between activities (for example, when one activity leads into another, or when information is shared between one activity and another) by drawing arrows or lines.

RELATIONSHIPS

STEP 6

Fine-tune. As the Process Flow-Chart takes shape, it is likely to bring to light some process issues (such as too many activities occurring simultaneously, or not enough time allocated to a phase, or the need to add other tasks or activities). Make adjustments as necessary to fine-tune the process design.

STEP 7

Share. Once the group has fine-tuned and agreed to the final Process Flow-Chart, transfer it to a smaller sheet of paper or another format that can be easily shared with others. It will be an effective tool for communicating the project's process and activities to others. Use it as an organizational tool and post it prominently in the local project area. As the project progresses, use the diagram to highlight where you are in the process. Keep it up to date to reflect any modifications.

A simplified process graphic can be used to explain the participatory planning process to team members, participants and other community residents.

FIGURE 4

A sample process flow-chart

Here is what a process flow-chart might look like for a one-year participation programme for developing a
Community Action Plan.

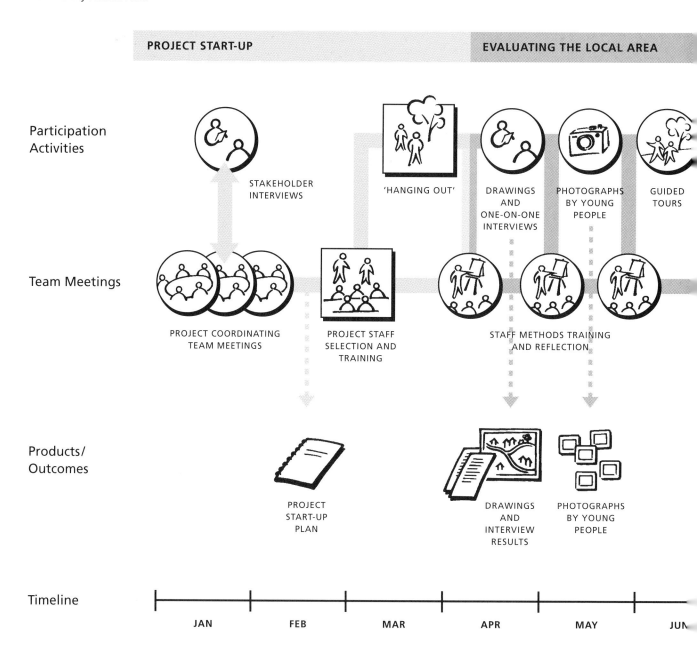

PROJECT START-UP

EVALUATING THE LOCAL AREA

Participation
Activities

STAKEHOLDER
INTERVIEWS

'HANGING OUT'

DRAWINGS
AND
ONE-ON-ONE
INTERVIEWS

PHOTOGRAPHS
BY YOUNG
PEOPLE

GUIDED
TOURS

Team Meetings

PROJECT COORDINATING
TEAM MEETINGS

PROJECT STAFF
SELECTION AND
TRAINING

STAFF METHODS TRAINING
AND REFLECTION

Products/
Outcomes

PROJECT
START-UP
PLAN

DRAWINGS
AND
INTERVIEW
RESULTS

PHOTOGRAPHS
BY YOUNG
PEOPLE

Timeline

JAN   FEB   MAR   APR   MAY   JUN

ANALYSING RESULTS/PLANNING FOR CHANGE

TAKING ACTION

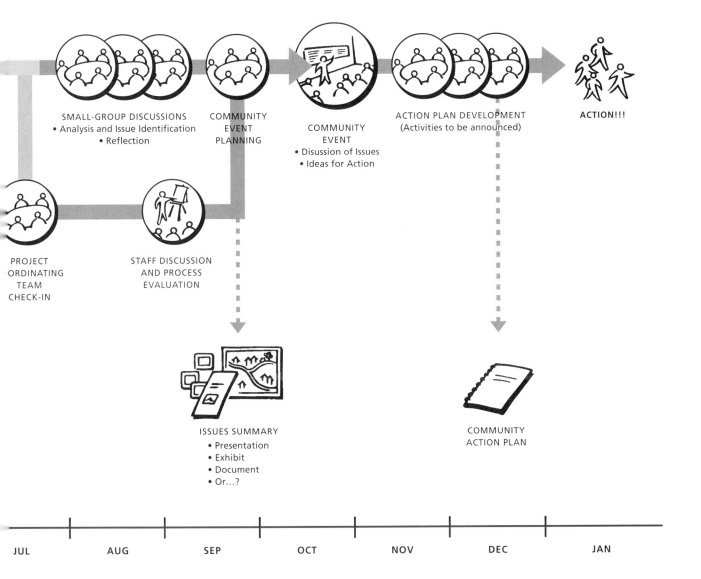

SMALL-GROUP DISCUSSIONS
• Analysis and Issue Identification
• Reflection

COMMUNITY
EVENT
PLANNING

COMMUNITY
EVENT
• Disussion of Issues
• Ideas for Action

ACTION PLAN DEVELOPMENT
(Activities to be announced)

ACTION!!!

PROJECT
CORDINATING
TEAM
CHECK-IN

STAFF DISCUSSION
AND PROCESS
EVALUATION

ISSUES SUMMARY
• Presentation
• Exhibit
• Document
• Or...?

COMMUNITY
ACTION PLAN

JUL	AUG	SEP	OCT	NOV	DEC	JAN

Choosing and Customising Participation Methods

Chapter 6 provides a 'toolkit' of different participation methods. Each method description provides an overview of its purpose and an explanation of how to implement it. It also provides examples of how the method can be adapted to various circumstances.

In determining which methods to use for your process design, and how they may need to be customised, consider the following questions:

> What is the method trying to achieve?
> How many people will be involved?
> What are their ages and abilities?
> How many project team members will be needed?
> What special materials will be needed?
> How much time is available?
> Where will the project take place?
> What other methods could achieve the same result?
> What issues might the method raise that will need to be addressed?

If you are using a method that is new to you or you are unsure whether a method will work in the context of the area where you are working, conduct a 'pre-test' with a small group of children of similar age and background outside the project area. This may lead to refinements in the method approach, or a decision to use a different method altogether.

AGE-APPROPRIATENESS

An effective participation programme provides multiple opportunities for input and involvement, allowing participants of all ages to choose the level and type of participation they prefer based on their ability, interest, and availability.

The competence of children (like the competence of adults) varies widely depending on how meaningful and familiar they find tasks to be. As children grow and develop, they are able to grasp and respond to issues of greater complexity and they become increasingly aware of and interested in the larger world around them. In general, as children grow older, they will:

> develop their ability to empathize and to understand and respond to moral issues.
> have greater access to the local environment, extending their territorial range further from home.
> develop a broader range of environmental interests and a capacity to understand increasingly complex environmental and ecological issues.
> develop stronger social skills and an understanding of themselves as part of a larger societal system.
> grow increasingly aware of political structures and processes, and develop a deeper understanding of issues of economic, social and environmental justice.

With this in mind, it is important that participation activities for young people be designed in a manner that is age-appropriate. Asking young people to undertake activities that are beyond their capacity will not benefit anyone. On the other hand, *children will often sur-*

prise you with their abilities and level of maturity. Think creatively about how to support young people's engagement at every age, and how to offer activities with graduated levels of difficulty. The limitations to children's participation are usually not their incapacity to understand and contribute, but adults' failure to discover appropriate ways to involve them.

The most reliable method for ensuring that project expectations and activities are age-appropriate is to involve the children themselves in defining the project's objectives and determining its activities. The adult facilitator must make sure that objectives and activities can be achieved within the overall constraints of the project.

© DAVID DRISKELL

© DAVID DRISKELL

A variety of activities allows children of different ages and abilities as well as their parents to participate in the process of designing a new play area. Very young children are engaged in fun activities that give them an opportunity to think and talk about possible play area features (below left), while older children build models to express their ideas (above). Youth and adults can also be involved in group discussions, as shown in the photograph on page 73.

Developing a Project Start-up Plan

A Project Start-up Plan can be used to guide project management and administration activities; to present the project to potential funding agencies; and to communicate the project's approach and parameters to the project team, participants and other members of the community.

A sample outline of a Project Start-up Plan is provided below. Depending on the situation, additional information may be required or a briefer version may be adequate. It can be presented as a typed, professional-looking document to share with potential funding agencies and local officials, or as a series of wallcharts hung in the room where the Project Coordinating Team, staff and participants meet.

Sample Outline of a Project Start-up Plan

1. Project context
- *Local issues and trends.* A brief overview of issues and trends that are impacting on young people in the local area.
- *Opportunities.* Summary of how a participatory project might capitalize on and respond to conditions and opportunities in the local area.
- *Potential barriers and constraints.* A realistic summary of factors that might present barriers to implementation of the project or constrain the scope of its activities, and how they might be managed or minimized.

2. Project definition
- *Goals and outcomes.* A statement of the pre-defined goals and expected outcomes for the project.
- *General setting.* Description of the general socio-economic group and the type of settlement or community on which the project will focus.
- *Site(s).* Description of the specific site or sites that have been or could be selected as the project's focus.
- *Key stakeholders.* A brief profile of the key groups and individuals that will be affected by or interested in the proposed project.

- *Child and youth participants.* An overview of the proposed child and youth participants, including the group size, ages, economic status and composition by gender, race, ethnicity, religion and/or language group, with special attention to any 'invisible' groups.

3. Logistics
- *Team organization.* Overview of the project's staffing resources, including paid staff, volunteers and/or staff from affiliated organizations.
- *Budget.* An estimate of the project's cost and the source or potential sources of funding, at an appropriate level of detail.
- *Project schedule and milestones.* An outline of the project's overall schedule and activities, identifying key milestones (with an estimated date for each).

4. Process design and first steps
- *Process flow-chart.* A graphic representation of the various project activities, showing both their sequencing and relative timing (see page 74).
- *Start-up tasks and schedule.* A detailed outline and schedule of the activities to be undertaken in getting the project under way.

ENDNOTES

[1] In 'Children's Rights and the Changing Face of Work in the Field', PLA Notes 25, p. 61, London, International Institute for Environment and Development, February 1996. Publication and contact information for PLA Notes can be found in Appendix B.

[2] For discussions of monitoring and reflection with children, see the special issue of PLA Notes on 'Children's Participation in Community Settings: Evaluating Effectiveness'. London, International Institute for Environment and Development, October 2001. Publication and contact information for PLA Notes can be found in Appendix B.

Getting Under Way

CHAPTER FIVE

Young people take
adult team members on
a walking tour of their
neighbourhood.

© NILDA COSCO

*A goods train won't move by my pushing it, or even by getting
ten others to help in pushing it. But our action may inspire
someone to get an engine.*

VINOO KALEY[1]

The initial phase of a project should be devoted to organizing and training the project staff, making initial contact with child and youth participants, and establishing the basic working structure for daily project operations.

This chapter provides an overview of the types of individuals who may be appropriate to involve in your project staff, as well as tips for working with young people and guidelines for dealing with basic organizational issues.

Organizing and Training Project Staff

Members of the staff team must be able to communicate clearly, listen carefully, be supportive, delegate authority, and allow young participants to play a real role in project decision-making. They must have skills in facilitation, mediation, staff training, financial management, and public communication. Last, and most important, they must have a keen interest in young people and a strong commitment to improving their lives. (The roles of the project staff are summarized in the box on page 83.)

This may sound like a great deal to ask of people on the project team, and it is. But one of the most fundamental truths of any participatory project is that success hinges first and foremost on the abilities, ideas, enthusiasm and commitment of its core staff members.

SELECTING PROJECT STAFF

Meet with potential staff members to explain the project, discuss what they can bring to the project, and define their roles. Whenever possible, youth and young adults should be included as staff members. Issues to consider in selecting project team members include:

- **Background and skills.** Include a mix of professionals and community members who represent the backgrounds, skills and perspectives that will be valuable for the project. Most of the sites in the GUIC project, for example, included a physical environment professional (such as an architect, planner or designer) and a social science researcher (such as an anthropologist, psychologist or educator) in addition to local community members. This combination of perspectives was extremely valuable in the project.
- **Experience.** Experience of working with young people is extremely valuable, especially when combined with openness to working in new ways. Experience of working in the local area can also be valuable, as long as preconceptions about community needs and issues do not get in the way.
- **Local politics.** Consider the political and other community affiliations of prospective team members. Knowledge and experience in local community politics can be an asset in seeking support for the project and implementation of proposals. However, if team members are from opposing political groups, internal conflicts may result.

- **Gender.** Cultural norms may dictate the need for female staff to work with girls and male staff to work with boys. But, in any culture, male staff may intimidate young girls and teenage boys may be uncomfortable interacting with female staff. It may therefore be important to have a mix of men and women on your project team. Do not rigidly assign roles based on gender, however. Individual personalities are the most important factor in determining compatibility. Allow children to work with the adults that they feel most comfortable with.

- **Attitude and demeanour.** Project staff must be able to relate well to young people, quickly winning their trust and confidence. They must enjoy working with young people, be good listeners, and be committed to responding to and following through on young people's ideas and input.

- **Language.** As a practical matter, project staff must be able to converse with young people in their everyday language. This may require recruiting staff fluent in multiple languages.

- **Ethnicity, caste or religion.** The ethnicity, caste or religion of staff and participants may be an issue in some cultural settings. Determine if it will be an issue at your site and whether it should be considered in the selection of project staff.

- **Commitment and enthusiasm.** The energy, enthusiasm and commitment of the staff are the factors that will sustain the project. Select individuals who are self-motivated and can work independently, but who are also team players. Most important, select those who genuinely care about young people and the local community.

© ROBIN MOORE

Experience, language, gender, and other factors are important considerations in staff selection. But most important is the individual's commitment, enthusiasm, and willingness to engage with young people as equals in the participatory process.

STAFF ORGANIZATION AND COMMUNICATION

The project team must be well organized, with clear communication between staff members as well as between staff and participants. Group conflict can result from overlapping or inadequately defined roles, or from misunderstandings and misconceptions arising from poor communication.

- **Role clarification.** Involve staff members in a discussion about the skills that each person brings to the project, the roles that each would like to play, and the responsibilities they must take on. Make sure everyone knows what their roles are, what tasks they are responsible for, and when they need to complete their tasks.

- **Respect, support and acknowledgement.** An important outcome of any participatory project is the increased skill level and awareness of project staff. When staff members feel positive about their experience, they are likely to advocate and apply participatory approaches in their future work. Each staff member needs to feel the support of the team, with his or her unique skills and contributions acknowledged and appreciated. No one person should be allowed to take credit for the project. Give credit where it is due, both in the work by the staff and by the community.

Initial meetings provide an opportunity to get to know each other as more than just names and job titles. Here, a workshop participant introduces herself with a poster collage that was made as an initial workshop activity. It illustrates her interests, experience, ideas and hopes for the future.

- **Collaboration and communication with other sites.** A key benefit of Growing Up in Cities was that teams from sites in different countries were able to meet at the start of the project as well as later, after the projects were under way. They were also able to keep in contact through e-mail, allowing teams to share problem-solving ideas and to celebrate each other's accomplishments. If other groups in your city, region or country are interested in child and youth participation, try to organize a group meeting to share ideas. This may result in a local, regional or national network of individuals, groups and agencies interested in participatory, community-based projects with young people. This can facilitate information-sharing and collaborative problem-solving, and help to develop the political support and institutional frameworks needed for implementation. A local website can also be established to facilitate communication and information sharing.

INITIAL STAFF MEETINGS

As soon as staff members are selected, hold an initial meeting. Topics to cover include:

> Roles and responsibilities of each staff person (see Figure 5).

> Individual project goals and expectations, and reasons for being involved.

> Importance of open and honest communication between all team members.

> General organization of activities. (How do you plan to divide the work? Will you all share equally in each part of the project, or will each member focus on specific tasks?)

> Expected project duration and level of time commitment.

> Ethical issues related to working with children and youth (see page 91).

> Project logistics, such as staff meetings; office rules and procedures; and filing systems.

These initial team meetings will help to set the tone for the rest of the project. Keep the group energized and emphasize the importance of open, honest communication.

FIGURE 5

Roles of project staff[2]

In a participatory project, staff members will play a variety of roles. These may be played by one person or by a group of people working together. It is not necessary or desirable to have one individual assigned to each role. Rather, staff members should be encouraged to play different roles based on their own strengths and desires.

Facilitator
- Make sure that all participants are involved and valued.
- Maintain a high energy level.
- Create a comfortable, creative atmosphere.
- Continually and consistently coordinate the group process to build solidarity and strong working relationships.
- Infuse new ideas when things slow down.
- Allow the group process or decision-making to emerge from the group.
- Ensure that group input and points of agreement are properly recorded.

Trainer
- Ensure that all members of the team are properly trained in the project's approach and methods.
- Incorporate opportunities for formal and informal learning in the participation process.
- Help to develop the local community's capacity for conducting community-based planning projects.

Mediator
- Ensure that all parties have a chance to voice their views and opinions.
- Create a non-judgemental atmosphere for creative problem-solving.
- Help to overcome disagreements through focused discussion.
- Intervene as necessary to resolve conflict.
- Identify areas of agreement and build consensus.
- Act as a neutral third party to assist in problem resolution.

Interpreter and resource person
- Open channels of communication.
- Help to explain complex ideas and technical data in a manner understood by all.
- Build bridges between the community and external resources.

Networker
- Build broad-based community support for the project and process.
- Involve potential supporters in the process.
- Create long-term strategic alliances for community change.

Project manager
- Manage the project's resources and ensure that deadlines are met.
- Ensure a process of systematic, comprehensive inquiry and detailed, structured documentation.
- Communicate project results and progress to external funding agencies.

Activist
- Ensure that the project's process and results benefit the community.
- Work with community members to act on the project's findings and implement positive change.
- Ensure that ownership of the project's process and results lies with the community.

Reflective practitioner
- Engage in a process of critical review and evaluation at project milestones.
- Encourage constructive criticism and dialogue among group members.
- Respond constructively to critical input from group members and the community.
- Remain dedicated to constantly refining and improving the community-based, participatory planning process.

TRAINING

The extent and focus of staff training depends on their level of experience in participatory projects with young people and the nature of the project. The size of the group will also be a factor in deciding how to structure the training programme.

© DAVID DRISKELL

This manual can be used to identify potential training topics and develop a training workshop agenda that responds to your project's needs. Make sure that all team members understand why the project is being undertaken and the basic principles of participatory development. Clearly communicate the project's process design and the roles of each staff member, helping everyone to understand how their role fits into the larger project framework.

Training sessions should include fieldwork in which project staff gain experience using participation methods with young people. However, these practice sessions should not be conducted with young people from the project site. This is intended as a learning experience for the staff, not as an actual participation activity for the project. Rather than working in the project area, make arrangements to conduct the training activities with young people from another area.

Consider opportunities for bringing others into the training process, especially potential volunteers, interested college students, and local residents who might benefit from the information being covered. This can help to extend the project's benefits and contribute to the process of community capacity building.

Training workshops should include opportunities for working with young people and testing different methods. Above, in an international workshop held in the Netherlands, a workshop participant from Rwanda interviews a young person about the area where he lives.

ONGOING PROJECT STAFF MEETINGS

The project staff should meet on a regular basis to monitor progress, coordinate tasks, clarify responsibilities and schedules, share ideas and respond to any issues or problems that might arise in the field. These meetings provide important opportunities for reflection on what is going well in the project and what could be done differently. Use them as problem-solving opportunities as well as for coordination. As in meetings with the community at large, make sure that every staff meeting has a clear agenda, and that it is facilitated and recorded. Confirm agreements among team members regarding next steps, and keep a record of those agreements for future reference.

Staff Training Workshop in Bangalore, India

© DAVID DRISKELL

At the Indian Growing Up in Cities site, the local staff were introduced to the project and its participatory methods through a two-day training workshop. Local university students and interested staff from NGOs and government departments were also invited to attend.

PHOTO LEFT: A workshop participant shares her most memorable childhood place with the group.

Environmental Autobiographies

One of the first workshop activities involved participants introducing themselves to each other through a brief 'environmental autobiography' exercise.[3] Each person was given a large sheet of paper and either crayons or markers, and was asked to make a drawing of a significant childhood place — a favourite, memorable, or special place where he or she enjoyed spending time. Each person then presented their drawing, talking about the characteristics of the place: what it looked like, how it felt, what they did there, how they went there, and if there were other people there.

This exercise reconnects adults with their childhood experience of the world and opens their minds to the wide range of places that can be important to young people, reminding them that such places are not limited to officially designated sites such as schools and playgrounds. It is also a useful tool for introducing participants to each other as unique individuals with interesting pasts and perspectives.

Methods Overview

The first workshop session introduced the purpose and approach of participatory work with children and youth. Participants were given an overview of the project's purpose and goals, and introduced to some of the participation methods that would be used. The second session was devoted to field visits in which workshop participants gained practical experience in participation techniques.

Field Exercise #1: Drawings and Interviews

The first field exercise focused on young people's drawings of the area where they live and one-to-one interviews about those drawings and related issues (see 'Interviews', page 103, and 'Drawings', page 115).

To practice these methods, an afternoon field trip to a nearby municipal school (far from the project site) was arranged, where the workshop organizers had agreed with the principal and teachers to conduct interviews with children aged 10 to 14.

The children were briefed on the purpose of the interviews beforehand and asked to volunteer if they were interested in participating. Teachers were asked to leave the children alone during the interviews, and not to encourage children beforehand to answer in any particular way (e.g. 'tell the visitors how much you enjoy your school').

It was assumed that the children would be unfamiliar and uncomfortable with the adult participants; therefore the drawing exercise was done first in small groups. As children finished their drawings, they discussed them with the adult participants in a one-to-one or two-to-one interview (depending on the child's preference), with adult participants using a short interview instrument developed specifically for the practice session.

When the interviews were completed, workshop participants gathered to share results and discuss what went well, what was problematic and what they would do differently in the future.

Field Exercise #2: Behaviour Mapping

The second field exercise focused on 'behaviour mapping' (page 134) — a systematic technique for documenting people's behaviour in the local environment. It also helped participants to develop their skills in observation, looking for physical signs in the environment that might indicate how the area is used and valued by children.

Workshop participants gained hands-on experience in drawings and interviews.

For this exercise participants visited a park located near the workshop site. Each participant was given a map of the park area, mapping instructions, clipboard, pen and an inexpensive camera. Working in teams of two or three, they spread out in the park area and spent an hour mapping activities. They also noted their observations about the use of different parts of the park and its physical characteristics, and documented the most important observations on film.

After the field exercise, participants reconvened and compared notes about what they had seen and learned. The workshop closed with the granting of certificates to all participants and an invitation to non-staff members to continue their participation in the project. Some of the university students who participated in the training responded to this invitation and later became volunteer assistants, providing valuable support in carrying out project activities.

Working with Young People

Participatory processes are sometimes criticized for taking too much time, especially when they involve young people. However, real participation requires the development of trust and respect between all participants. Be sure to give adequate time and effort to establishing contact with young people and building rapport with them *before* attempting any substantive participation activities.

MAKING CONTACT

If the project area is unfamiliar or you lack relationships with the young people there, you will need to decide how best to make initial contact and build their interest in the project.

The following are some suggestions:

- **Go through adult members of the community.** Ask adult residents or community leaders to introduce you to young people in the target age group. Use these introductions as a means of getting to know an initial group of young people, and through them their friends and extended peer network. Before long, you will have made personal contact with a substantial number of young people in the area.

- **Hang out.** This is often the most effective way of getting to know young people, in settings where they are most comfortable. Depending on the community, it may be difficult to just show up one day and start hanging out with young people. Some level of introduction within the community and with local youth will be necessary first. But once those introductions are made, the best way for building rapport is to spend time in young people's own places.

'Hanging out' can be an important activity for building comfort and trust with young people. See the discussion on page 99.

- **Get involved in youth-oriented community activities.** This provides a useful and productive vehicle for meeting young people. For example, in the Australian Growing Up in Cities project of the 1970s, researcher Peter Downton and other team members strengthened their relationships with local youth by volunteering to be drivers for young people going to a local summer camp. On the way to and from the camp they were able to engage in conversation, getting to know them in an informal and comfortable setting. By the end of their tour as chauffeurs, they had developed a much stronger rapport with the young participants, which benefited the subsequent participation activities.[4]

- **Sponsor a youth-oriented community event.** If there are no existing community-based youth activities, consider creating an activity or event that will attract young people and get them interested in the project. A day of activities in a local setting frequented by young people can achieve many purposes: attract potential participants; communicate the project's goals and purposes; and even implement some of the project's participatory components.

- **Go through the local schools.** This can be an effective and efficient method for approaching young people, although it can also be problematic if young people have a negative view of their school. Try to identify a local principal or teacher who is enthusiastic about the project and ask them to help you to find an opportunity to meet young people and introduce them to the project. These educators may become valuable partners in carrying out the project and implementing its findings. However, be sensitive to signs of distrust between young people and school officials, and consider whether some groups of young people may be left out of the process if it is focused too heavily on schools. If this is the case, try to distinguish between the project and other school activities, moving the project's activities into a non-school setting once introductions have been made.

BUILDING RAPPORT

Adults often forget what it was like to interact with older people as a young person. Few young people feel completely comfortable around adults, and even fewer will quickly and easily tell adults what they truly think and feel.

Spending time with young people in the places where they feel most comfortable can help build rapport.

Meaningful participation requires that adults build relationships of familiarity, trust and respect with young people. As young people begin to feel comfortable with adult members of the project team and see those adults as people who care about them, believe in them and want to help them, then young people will begin to express their views and ideas in more direct and honest ways.

Building rapport may require that adult staff members spend time with young people at the project site doing activities that are not directly related to any of the participatory methods, or using methods at the beginning of the project that are more informal or fun. 'Informal observations' and 'Hanging out' (page 99) and 'Photographs by young people' (page 130) are examples of methods that can be less threatening to young people and used to help to build rapport.

Whatever method is used, the important thing to remember is that young people must feel comfortable with adult project staff before any meaningful participation can begin. Take the time to get to know them and for them to get to know you. You cannot meet young people for the first time and expect that they will answer questions about their lives, opinions and ideas.

A summer program provides an opportunity to engage both young people and their parents

The Growing Up in Cities project in Saida, Lebanon, utilized an existing summer program for youth as the starting point for introducing young people to the project and exploring their perceptions and use of the local environment. The popular program, sponsored by the Hariri Foundation, had established rapport with many of the young people residing in the Old City. Building on this trust, one of the project team leaders suggested to the children that they take him and a small group of friends to their homes. One at a time, they organized several home visits to discuss the project, the parents' concerns, and their ideas related to their children's use of the Old City. The trips turned into challenges in map-making and map-reading because the children first had to make a map of how to go from the project centre to home, and the project leader and other children had to find their way by following the map. These initial home visits were enjoyable for both children and parents, and provided an opportunity to learn about the concerns of parents who would be unlikely to attend a public meeting.

© HARIRI FOUNDATION

A popular summer program in the Old City of Saida provided a starting point for working with young people on GUIC-related projects.

WORKING AS PARTNERS

For many people, working with young people in a participatory process is a new and challenging experience. It can also be a rich and rewarding experience, if approached with enthusiasm, openness and commitment. To achieve success, work with young people as partners rather than as objects of the community-development process.

The following are some basic ideas to help ensure that work with young people is positive, productive and mutually rewarding.

- **Treat young people with respect.** Children and youth, like adults, have the right to be treated fairly and ethically, to have their privacy respected, and to have the option of choosing not to participate.

- **Establish realistic expectations; do not raise false hopes.** Work with young people to establish realistic project objectives and communicate project constraints honestly and openly. Do not lead participants to believe that change will happen overnight. Focus on small, achievable goals.

- **Follow through on commitments, and expect the same in return.** Do not make promises you cannot keep. Be honest with yourself about the time and energy you have for the project, communicate your limitations, and then follow through on the commitments you have made. Likewise, help young people to define their own roles and responsibili-

At the South African GUIC site, project leaders and participants would meet in a circle every morning to review the day's activities and agree on the basic ground rules. This regular reiteration of the group's rules and orientation to each day's expectations helped to facilitate a smoother group process.

ties related to the project, and then through your example and encouragement help them to keep the commitments they have made.

- **Respect their other time commitments.** Like adults, young people have many responsibilities and commitments. They also need time to themselves. Structure the project and its activities in order not to conflict with participants' other commitments (school activities, family holidays, mealtimes, etc.).

- **Create an atmosphere of respect, cooperation, patience and creativity.** Work with participants to establish basic ground rules for group conduct (for example: 'all ideas are valid', 'there are no wrong questions', 'everyone has a right to be heard', 'no name-calling'). Ask the group to respect these rules and to monitor their enforcement. If conflicts arise or rules are broken (as they are bound to be at some point in any group), be prepared to take on the role of mediator and help the group to find a resolution.

- **Establish openness, transparency and trust.** Young people should understand the basic project boundaries, including its goals, expected outcomes, and process design. They should also understand the roles of the various team players, as well as their own responsibilities as participants. Within this 'transparent' environment, backed by open communication and trust, children are better able to develop a sense of confidence in their ability to speak and be heard. Over time, they also learn to test the project's established boundaries, pushing beyond into new realms of participation.[5]

- **Meet where young people are comfortable.** Conduct project activities in an environment where young people feel comfortable and 'in charge'. This might be an outdoor space (weather permitting), a youth club or other facility that young people have made their own. Schools, offices and even community centres are often places where young people feel less comfortable, since they are places of adult authority.

- **Maximize opportunities for 'real power'.** Young people need to have ownership of their ideas and to participate fully in overcoming the project's challenges and enjoying its successes. They must be given opportunities to participate in decision-making, as well as the time and space to develop their own ideas apart from adult supervision. If young people are given a space to work in — which is under their control — they are more likely to develop a sense of efficacy, which will extend into other aspects of the project.[6]

Participation activities should be fun for everyone, regardless of age. However, for young children, participation activities can be structured as games or play activities, providing opportunities for input and discussion with older youth and adults in the process.

- **Encourage reflection and self-evaluation.** Young people should be encouraged to re-flect on the project and their own participation, thinking about what they learned, what they accomplished, what they did not accomplish, and what they think they would do differently if given the chance.

- **Express your appreciation and give them the credit they deserve.** Make sure young participants know that their time, energy and input are appreciated. Give them proper credit in all reports, publications, presentations and other materials that are generated through the project.

- **Make it fun.** Use approaches that are playful and fun. This is often listed as a major motivating factor for young people. Participation can be a bridge to new friendships or to interacting with friends in new ways. Keep a sense of humour and playful attitude in your project work, making it an enjoyable learning experience that young people will want to do again.

At the South African GUIC site, playleaders led group games and activities to provide a fun atmosphere and diversion for participants while one-to-one or small group discussions were taking place with others.

Ethical Issues

The process of working with young people raises ethical issues that need to be understood and taken seriously by all adults. The nature of adult/youth relationships is that adults have power, and children and youth do not. Similarly, outsiders entering a lower-income or marginalised community may bring with them, consciously or unconsciously and whether they like it or not, a history of class, race or other relationships that probably place them in a position of power in relation to the local community.

These lopsided power relationships will be a significant issue in all your work. The worst thing to do is pretend they do not exist, or that you are somehow different and these issues therefore do not apply. Issues of power do not only come from how you act as an individual, but how you (or your organization or agency) are perceived by others.

The following basic guidelines are intended to help establish and sustain ethical working relationships between adults and young people and between outsiders and local communities.

- **Be aware of the issue of power in all interactions.** Serious ethical issues are much more likely to arise in a situation where people fail to acknowledge the existence of lop-sided relationships or think that somehow such imbalanced relationships will not impact on their work.

- **Acknowledge and respect the rights and responsibilities of all participants.** This is an essential ingredient to a successful participation process, as well as a foundation for ethical relationships. This includes respecting people's privacy and confidentiality; respecting their other commitments and responsibilities (each person must be free to make his or her own decision about how much time to give to the project); and respecting their right to participate or not in project activities, as they choose. It also means respecting people's right of ownership on the contributions they make to the project. If you plan to use a drawing, map or idea developed by someone else, you should obtain their permission and give them proper credit.

- **Establish open, honest communication and transparency in the group process.** Everyone should be made aware of what is being done in the project, and why. There should be no hidden agendas, ulterior motives or coercion.

- **Do not tolerate abusive relationships.** It should be made clear to all participants from the beginning of the project that there will be no tolerance of abusive relationships. Sexual abuse, harassment, coercion, rudeness and other forms of abuse are absolutely counter to the goals and values of participation.

- **Provide a clearly defined process for people to air their grievances about the project or specific relationships within it.** All participants should be made aware of their rights and responsibilities, and where to go if they feel that those rights and responsibilities (theirs or someone else's) are being ignored. There should be more than one person to whom participants can go for help, and those people should be properly trained in how to deal with potential issues. When grievances are expressed, they should be dealt with seriously and resolved promptly.

- **Involve young people in discussions regarding ethical issues.** In the spirit of openness and transparency, and to provide a valuable group opportunity for learning and sharing, involve young people in discussions and decisions related to ethical issues. For example, work together to establish group rules for the project, defining basic rights and responsibilities, agreeing on the best ways to ensure open communication, and identifying ways to avoid and address abusive or inappropriate relationships.

The choice about confidentiality is for young people to make. In some Growing Up in Cities sites, children's identities were kept completely confidential, while in others children chose a 'nickname' to use as their identity. In some sites, children chose to be referred to by their real names in project documents.

CONFIDENTIALITY

Establish a clear policy regarding confidentiality and communicate that policy to all participants. Whenever possible, involve young people in defining the project's confidentiality policy. If the project involves an organization with pre-set confidentiality requirements (as is often the case for university research projects), be sure to communicate these requirements to the participants.

In some situations, young people may want complete confidentiality and anonymity in order to speak their minds freely. This may include having a quiet, private place in which to conduct interviews or carry out project-related conversations. In other situations, they may want to use the project as a vehicle for having their voices heard directly by adult decision-makers, with their input and comments attributed to them by name. A middle-ground approach may involve young people in selecting an assumed identity or nickname to be used in project documents and presentations.

FIGURE 6

Consent forms

A common practice in many participatory research projects is to ask participants to sign a 'consent form' giving their permission to be photographed and/or identified in project documents. This helps to ensure that participants are informed about the possibility of being photographed in the project and that they consent to the possibility of their picture appearing in publications. Ideally, consent forms should be signed at the beginning of the project, but only *after* you have established a comfortable rapport with young people and their parents. Following is a typical consent form statement.

I, _____ [PERSON'S NAME], *agree to participate in*
_____ [PROJECT'S NAME]. *I understand that photographs may be taken of me during the course of the project, and that these may appear in published documents related to the project. I hereby consent to be photographed and authorize the use of photographs bearing my image in publications and other materials related to the project.*

When referring to me in any documents, I request that the project:

◯ *Use my actual name,* _____

◯ *Refer to me by the assumed name of* _____

CHILD'S SIGNATURE _____ DATE _____

PARENTS' SIGNATURES _____ DATE _____

Although consent forms are important to have in many settings with children, they are never a substitute for ongoing communication and discussion about the project goals and participants' feelings about their involvement. Also, it is critical that participants who do not wish to sign a consent form have their wishes respected, and that their participation should not be curtailed in any way as a result.

Keeping Things Organized

It is extremely important that the information gathered by the project be carefully documented, organized and archived to provide a record of the process, input and decisions.

FIELD NOTES AND MATERIALS

Set up a workable system of organizing and filing the information generated through the project. This will require a fair amount of effort at the beginning to establish the system, and some time spent every day in implementing and managing it. If you let files get disorganized, you run the risk of losing valuable information, and may end up spending more time reorganizing than if you had done it right from the beginning.

Some general notes follow for setting up and managing a workable system of filing and organization. These have been provided by Robin Moore, co-leader of Growing Up in Cities in Argentina and a seasoned field researcher.

- **Interview records** (page 103). Keep originals in three-ring binders. File interview responses, time-activity records, and any other notes or materials in alphabetical order by last name. If conducting interviews with multiple groups (e.g. children, parents, officials), print the forms for each group on different-coloured paper to distinguish them from one another. Allocate an identification number to each individual for ease of reference and to preserve anonymity. Also, be sure to number, date, and title any audiotapes of interviews, and file them separately.

    Make a copy of each set of responses, and use this as a working copy. Store the originals in a separate location for security, and use the working copies during the analysis phase. This allows for cutting up the responses to open-ended questions and shuffling them to identify key themes and generate categories of responses.

- **Children's drawings** (page 115). Number, name and date each drawing for easy reference and future credit. Store the drawings flat in a simple folder made from a large sheet of stiff paper or 'ticket board' folded down the centre.

- **Focus-group and small-group discussion records** (page 147). File the typed transcripts from focus-group sessions in a separate binder. Make working copies and store the originals in a safe place. Number, date and title any audiotapes and file separately.

- **Slides, negatives and prints.** Develop separate systems for each set of photographs: photos from walking tours; observation photos; photos of meetings, workshops, or special events; child-taken photos. When appropriate, include a map with each set of photos to key the locations and perspectives of each photo.

    It is extremely important that visual information such as prints and slides be properly organized and maintained. These can quickly get out of control, and irreplaceable data will be damaged, destroyed or misplaced. Photographs, negatives, contact sheets and slides should be catalogued, labelled (with name, date and location) and filed *immediately* after they return from processing.

Be sure to properly file and store negatives. Do not just throw them all in a shoebox! Plastic sleeves, designed specifically for storing photographs, slides and negatives, can be found at most camera-supply or film-processing stores. To store photographs, negatives or slides for a long period of time, invest in 'archival quality' file pages. These are made from a polypropylene plastic that will not cause prints to yellow over time.

A digital camera can help to reduce or eliminate the need for special archival storage. However, it is still essential to (a) keep photographs organized in a logical filing system on your computer; (b) maintain a consistent file-naming system; and (c) keep a back-up of digital photos on a disk stored in a safe place (i.e. at a different location from the main computer). If possible, scan hard-copy images (traditional prints, slides or negatives) into a digital format and store in a similar manner.

PROCESS DOCUMENTATION

Be sure to document the project's process as well as its results. Take photographs of participatory activities (interviews, meetings, workshops, walking tours, etc.) and of the team in action (preparing materials, discussing strategy, conducting training, analysing results). Take notes on how the process was organized and on the evaluation of what worked as well as what did not. Document the ways in which methods were modified, and describe new methods and activities that were developed.

Process records will prove valuable over time when undertaking new projects or when explaining the project to other groups. They can also be used to develop short articles for publication, helping others to learn from your experiences.

Photographic images should be coded and filed immediately after processing. The Growing Up in Cities site in India coded each roll of film that was processed, recording the name of the photographer and date with each set of negatives. Information about specific photos was also recorded.

ENDNOTES

1 Quoted in Rajni Bakshi, *Bapu Kuti: Journeys in Rediscovery of Gandhi*, New Delhi, Penguin Books, 1998.

2 Adapted in part from Amy Kaspar, *'Looking Out': Lessons and Visions for Young People's Participation in the Urban Built Environment*, p. 71, Oxford, Oxford Brookes University, 1997.

3 The idea of an 'environmental autobiography' is to reflect on the places where you spent time growing up, and how your experiences in and of those places shaped your relationship to the world around you and your personal development. The example here is a very simple and brief exercise, used to introduce participants to each other and to some of the basic project concepts (i.e. that the physical environment plays an important role in the life of a child, and that the environments we typically label as being 'for children' — such as school yards and playgrounds — are often not the environments that are most highly valued by children, including by ourselves when we were children). A more in-depth 'environmental autobiography' exercise may be worthwhile for adult team members who wish to better understand their own environmental experiences and biases, helping them to develop a more complete appreciation of the role of the physical environment in the lives of children.

4 Karen Malone, Lindsay Hasluck, and Beau B. Beza, *Growing Up in Cities, Braybrook Report 1997*, Deakin University, University of Melbourne. Australian Institute for Family Studies, and EDAW (Aust.), Pty. Ltd., 1997.

5 Kaspar, op. cit., p. 69.

6 Ibid.

Participation Toolkit

6

Young people in Buenos Aires
interview an adult resident
of their neighbourhood.

© ROBIN MOORE

*The things that hurt one do not show on a map. The truth of a
place is in the joy and hurt that come from it.*

MODUPE[1]

This chapter provides an overview of participatory methods that can be used to involve young people in looking at and evaluating their local environment. These methods have proved valuable in a variety of sites in countries and cultures around the world.

The chapter does not contain all possible methods, nor is it an exhaustive treatment of each. It should be used as a starting point and a resource base from which to develop participatory tools that make sense for your site and situation. Examples from the Growing Up in Cities sites are provided to illustrate how basic methods can be modified in response to local issues and needs. The basic methods included are:

A young girl in Bangalore, India, makes a drawing of the area where she lives.

- **Informal Observations and 'Hanging Out'** (PAGE 99)
- **Interviews** (PAGE 103)
- **Drawings** (PAGE 115)
- **Daily Activity Schedules** (PAGE 118)
- **Family and Support Networks** (PAGE 121)
- **Role-Play, Drama and Puppetry** (PAGE 124)
- **Guided Tours** (PAGE 127)
- **Photographs by Young People** (PAGE 130)
- **Behaviour Mapping** (PAGE 134)
- **Questionnaires and Surveys** (PAGE 139)
- **Focus Groups and Small-Group Discussions** (PAGE 147)
- **Workshops and Community Events** (PAGE 154)

Each method is written and formatted as a self-contained description. This results in some redundancy if you are reading the methods in sequence. However, it makes it possible to photocopy and distribute the individual method descriptions for training sessions and group discussions.

The following topics are included in each method: 'Purpose', 'Time required', 'Materials needed', 'Maximizing young people's participation' and 'Process guide'. This information, along with that in Chapter 4 (Designing the Process), can be used to determine the sequence of methods that is appropriate for your site.

METHOD

Informal Observations and 'Hanging Out'

Informal observations provide valuable anecdotal information as well as information about specific events or activities in the local area. Observations should be noted in project journals along with daily comments on the project's process and related evaluation notes, providing a written record of what happened during the course of the project. Although this is not a participatory method per se, it can be made participatory by having young people themselves record their daily observations in individual project journals.

Related to informal observations, spending unstructured time at the site, or 'hanging out', can help to reveal young people's perspectives on and use of the local area. It can also increase young people's level of comfort and trust with adult team members, opening doors for better communication and developing the relationships necessary for meaningful youth participation.

PURPOSE

> Document use of the local area.
> Build rapport by spending unstructured time at the site.
> Confirm or clarify issues identified through other methods.

TIME REQUIRED

> *Informal observations:* Minimal to moderate time required. Training on the use of a project journal can be valuable. Time spent in recording daily observations will vary from 5 to 20 minutes, on average.

> *'Hanging out':* Potentially significant, depending on the circumstances and need for developing familiarity and trust between participants and adult team members. Could vary from a day or two to several weeks.

'Hanging out' is an important social activity for many young people and can provide an opportunity for informal interaction and rapport-building.

© BARRY PERCY-SMITH

MATERIALS NEEDED

> Diary or project journal
> Pen or pencil
> Camera and film (or disks) — see 'Using a camera', page 102

The value of 'hanging out'

Some of the richest and most insightful information from the Growing Up in Cities site in India was collected over the course of a month during which the project was interrupted for a number of political and administrative reasons. During this period, one of the project's staff members spent considerable time at the site with young people — playing with them, engaging in conversations, and getting to know them better. As he developed a rapport with some of the local boys, they began to introduce him to some of their 'secret places' — places where they went to get away from parental authority and engage in a variety of play activities. These were places unmentioned in the previous project interviews, yet were of great significance in the children's daily lives. This information — and many of the insights that followed — might have remained undiscovered without the time spent 'just hanging out'.

MAXIMIZING YOUNG PEOPLE'S PARTICIPATION

> *Provide journals for young participants.* Encourage young people to keep their own daily journal of the things they see and do in their local area.

> *Share experiences.* Engage young people in small-group discussions about the things they have recorded in their journals and what insights they have gained about their area. Share the entries and insights from the journals of adult team members too.

PROCESS GUIDE

1. **'Hang out'.** This involves spending unstructured time with small groups of young people in the local area. For some adults and in some locations, this may be an easy and natural activity. For others, it may take more effort or creativity to overcome barriers based on age or other factors. 'Working with young people' on page 87 provides examples of ways to make contact and build rapport. Regardless of your situation, be sure to:
   • Let people in the community (young and old) know what you are doing and why you are there.
   • Devote adequate time to rapport building before trying to engage young people in more participatory activities.

2. **Conduct training.** Train project staff members and participants to pay close attention to the relationship between what is happening, where it is happening, and why. Questions to consider include:
   • What types of activity are taking place (active group play, a conversation between friends, children at work, shopping…)?
   • Who is involved (only older children, all age groups, only boys, only girls…)?

- Where is the activity taking place (in the street, in front of the home, in a garden...)?
- Is there a reason why the activity is there and not somewhere else (in the shade, hidden from view, in a busy area...)?
- What day of the week is it?
- What time of day is it?
- What is the duration of the activity?

3. **Keep project journals.** Encourage project staff members and participants to keep a journal in which they document their activities, experiences, observations, perspectives and insights. Encourage everyone to share excerpts from their journals with each other periodically over the course of the project to see if recurrent or varying observations are being recorded, and if informal observations are consistent with other information being gathered. Journal entries can include sketches and photographs as well as words.

Observations over time help to understand the way that children's use of the local environment changes according to the season. This child-taken photo from the GUIC site in Trondheim, Norway, shows a playground and football field that are popular in summer for outdoor play and then maintained as an area for ice skating in the winter.

Observing seasonal changes in place use

The Trondheim, Norway, GUIC site provides an excellent example of the value of informal observations in understanding the seasonal changes in children's use of their local environment. By recording observations of children's behaviour on a regular basis over the course of the project, team members were able to document and better understand the changing nature of children's outdoor play and use of space, supplementing the interviews, drawings and other methods that tended to provide more of a snapshot in time of how children were using space during the particular season of the year.

Informal Observations
and 'Hanging Out'

Using a camera

A camera can be a valuable tool for documenting information about a place, its people, and their activities. However, the use of a camera can also create obstacles to effective communication. The following are some factors to consider when deciding whether or not to use cameras:

PROS

- **A picture says a thousand words.** A well-taken spontaneous photograph can be a powerful and insightful communication tool.
- **Valuable documentation.** Combined with notes in the project journal, a quick photograph can be a valuable data source.

CONS

- **Barrier to communication.** A camera (no matter how simple) is a sign of wealth in some communities and may be considered 'foreign' or regarded with suspicion. In these cases, a camera may be a barrier to effective communication rather than a tool in support of it.
- **Unwelcome intrusion.** In some cultures, people may be very sensitive to having their photograph taken. They may regard it as an invasion of their privacy.
- **Significant disruption.** When working in areas where a camera is a novelty — and especially when working with young people — the act of pulling out a camera is likely to be disruptive, altering the very activity or behaviour being documented (resulting in posed rather than authentic photographs).

The decision to use cameras should be made in consultation with the project staff and local residents. If the group decides to use cameras, there should be clear guidelines for when and how they are used — or not used, as the case may be.

One alternative to consider is having a skilled outside photographer come in for one or two days after project members have gained the children's and community's trust. This alternative was used effectively by the South African GUIC site and thus avoided project facilitators having to be photographers, which could lead to many of the problems listed above.

A camera need not be elaborate or expensive to be effective. Inexpensive reloadable cameras are recommended as they do not cost more than 'disposable' cameras, are simple to use, can be used repeatedly, and are more environmentally friendly. Simple digital cameras, while not inexpensive, can also be useful, reducing film development costs.

Taking photographs also raises ethical issues and the need for 'consent forms', as discussed on pages 91–93.

Interviews

Interviews are useful information-gathering tools, providing a systematic approach for getting input from young people (and other members of the community) as well as an opportunity for one-to-one interaction. But they also take time, requiring the project team to develop and test the 'interview instrument', schedule and conduct each interview, and sort through, analyse and summarize the results. However, despite the time required, *interviews were consistently ranked by the Growing Up in Cities teams as one of the most valuable information-gathering techniques.*

© DAVID DRISKELL

NOTE: For an explanation of the difference between an interview, a survey and a question-naire, see page 140.

Although they are time-consuming, interviews provide opportunities to understand each child's unique circumstances and perspectives.

PURPOSE

> Collect information directly from young people or others.
> Explore opinions and perspectives on key issues and questions.
> Spend time one-to-one with individual participants.

TIME REQUIRED

A minimum of one week will be required to prepare, pre-test and finalize the interview instrument, followed by 30 to 60 minutes per interview, or longer. Additional time will be needed to complete and organize notes immediately following each interview.

MATERIALS NEEDED

> Copies of the interview instrument
> Pens/pencils
> Clipboard or other writing surface
> Map or aerial photo of the local area (optional, but very useful)
> Tape recorder, with tapes and batteries (optional) — see page 107

Interviews

MAXIMIZING YOUNG PEOPLE'S PARTICIPATION

> *Conduct child-led conversations first.* Engage young people in 'unstructured interviews' (see page 108) early in the process to develop rapport, understand the context more fully, and identify key issues to explore in subsequent structured interviews.

> *Involve young people in developing the interview instrument.* Older youth can be involved in developing and testing the interview instrument, helping to make sure that questions are appropriately worded and key topics are not overlooked. Conduct a small group discussion to identify the interview topics, develop draft questions, and review the draft interview instrument.

> *Involve young people as evaluators.* Involve young people from the local area in evaluating the interview instrument and giving feedback on the interviewing skills of project team members.

> *Train young people as interviewers.* When older youth are part of the project team, they can be trained to interview younger children or peers. Their special rapport may help to ensure a successful interview process. Older youth can also develop their own interview instruments to collect information from peers, parents, decision-makers or local officials. As with adult interviewers, proper training is essential to ensure consistency in the interview process and meaningful results.

PHOTO RIGHT: Young people can interview their peers to explore issues of concern and ensure a broad range of perspectives.

© KAREN MALONE

PROCESS GUIDE

1. **Develop the interview instrument.** This is the set of questions to be used in the interviews. It provides a guide for the interviewer in terms of the questions to ask, and may also include instructional notes on how to conduct specific parts of the interview. The interview instrument also provides space for taking notes during each interview. See 'Developing an interview instrument' on page 109.

2. **Pre-test the instrument.** Use the draft interview instrument to interview several young people who are not from the local area but are similar in their background and experience to the group with whom you will be working. This pre-testing allows you to see if there are any points of confusion and if the questions lead to the type of information and feedback sought. It will also give project team members a chance to practice doing interviews. Interviewers can also gain experience by interviewing each other, providing insights into which questions work well, and which do not.

3. **Refine the instrument.** Based on the pre-test, refine the instrument to delete, add, re-word, or re-sequence questions as necessary. If the interview is long, consider reducing it or breaking it into two or more shorter interviews to keep children from becoming bored or tired (the interviews in the Growing Up in Cities project were divided into two sessions). If substantial modifications are made, another round of pre-testing is needed before beginning the interviews.

4. **Train the interviewers.** For the interviews to be a meaningful source of information, all interviewers must be properly trained. They must be familiar with the interview instrument; comfortable with young people; capable of taking complete, accurate and comprehensible notes; and able to prompt and ask follow-up questions without inserting their own biases and perspectives. The pre-test phase is an excellent opportunity to conduct team training on interview techniques and to test interview skills. See 'Being an effective interviewer' (page 112) as well as the example of an interview training session at the Indian GUIC site (page 85).

5. **Accommodate children with special needs.** Consider the special needs of young people who might otherwise be excluded or marginalized in the interview process. For example, those with limited hearing may require a sign-language interpreter, while those with limited mobility will need to meet in an accessible location. Young people who work may require scheduling flexibility or an interview that is less time-intensive. See 'Extending the participatory process to children with special needs' on page 58.

6. **Find a suitable location.** The interview should be conducted one-to-one, in a place that affords some degree of privacy (away from parents and other adults). Look for a place that is familiar, informal and neutral (preferably outside of school), as well as free from distractions and disruptions. If the only option is to conduct interviews in the street, try to find a quiet corner in which interruptions will be minimal. A local café where young people congregate can also be a suitable place to meet.

7. **Establish a realistic schedule.** Conduct all the interviews within a reasonable time span to minimize the variations that will undoubtedly come with changes in the season and time of year (for example, children's daily schedules will change considerably when school is out of session).

8. **Schedule the interviews.** Contact the young people to be interviewed and schedule an interview time. Explain to them why you want to meet, for how long, and what they can expect during the interview. Do not coerce them into being interviewed if they do not want to be, and make it clear that their answers will be kept confidential.

   For multiple-session interviews, schedule and conduct the follow-up interview within two to three days of the first interview (preferably the following day). If too many days pass between the interviews, it will be difficult to make references to the first interview as the details of the earlier conversation may have faded.

9. **Prepare the interview materials.** Organize the necessary materials (see 'Materials Needed' on page 103). Have a separate copy of the interview instrument for each interview to use for taking notes. A map or an aerial photo can be very engaging for young people and a great tool for identifying issues and opportunities in the local area.

10. **Get acquainted.** Spend time building rapport with young people before trying to engage them in interviews. Most young people will feel uncomfortable speaking with an adult they do not know and as a result their comments will be incomplete or inaccurate.

11. **Conduct the interviews.** Begin and end the interview on time. Start with a brief introduction, explaining that the purpose of the interview is to find out how young people use the place where they live and what they think about it. Ask their permission to proceed and to make notes or tape-record the interview for future reference (see 'Using a tape recorder' on the next page). During the interview, give periodic assurance that their responses are useful and appreciated. Avoid introducing other people into the conversation.

    If they become too tired or bored to continue with the interview, take a short break. If necessary, take a longer break and pick up the remaining interview questions at a later time that day or the following day.

12. **Take complete and accurate notes.** During the interview, take as complete and accurate notes as possible. *Immediately after each interview,* spend time reviewing, organizing and expanding the interview notes. Always strive to capture comments using young people's own words. For this purpose, it is extremely helpful to tape-record the interviews, though this can also be problematic, as discussed on the next page. If it is not possible to tape the interviews, then take detailed, careful notes that capture not only the substance of responses, but also the flavour of the discussion and salient quotations.

13. **Organize your records on a daily basis.** At the end of each interview day, properly label, file and store the results of that day's work.

14. **Summarize and analyse the results.** When summarizing the interview results, be sure to note the start-date and end-date for the interviews. Also, be sure to mark the interview reference number on each page of the instrument. In the process of analysing results, it will probably be easiest to take pages apart and sort them by question and response. If pages are not marked, it will be impossible to know which responses came from which interviewee. See page 162 for other recommendations on 'Analysing the results'. Also, be sure to consider the issue of confidentiality, discussed on page 92.

Using a tape recorder

Consider whether it is appropriate to use a tape recorder in project activities. The decision to use tape recorders should be discussed with the project staff and local residents. If the group decides to use tape recorders, there should be clear guidelines for when and how they are used, or not used. Factors to consider include:

PROS

- **In their own words.** A tape recorder captures people's comments in their own words, without the intervening and often distorting filter of the interviewer's shorthand notes and recollection.

- **Reliable record.** A taped interview provides a permanent, reliable record of what was said, making it possible to check and confirm specific statements.

CONS

- **Barrier to communication.** A tape recorder is a sign of wealth in some communities, and may be considered 'foreign' or regarded with suspicion. In these cases, a tape recorder may be a barrier to effective communication during the interview.

- **Unwelcome intrusion.** Some people may be very sensitive to having their interview recorded. It may make them uncomfortable, and unwilling to speak freely.

- **Time commitment.** Transcribing interview results from a tape can be very time-consuming and cumbersome. Skilled interviewers can save time by making notations during the interview (noting the number on the tape counter) of moments when the interviewee says something important or representative in a particularly clear or engaging way. It is then possible to go back and transcribe only those exact comments rather than the entire interview.

When used creatively, tape recorders may actually facilitate communication. For example, young people can use a tape recorder to conduct news-style interviews with each other or to develop a 'radio programme' about their local area or aspects of their lives.

Interviews

'Unstructured interviews' or child-led conversations

The interview method described on these pages focuses on 'structured interviews', a systematic approach to one-to-one discussions that allows you to compare the responses from numerous participants to the same set of questions. In an 'unstructured interview' or child-led conversation, there is no set list of questions that must be answered. Instead, the interviewer and respondent engage in a dialogue that begins at a general level and then focuses more specifically on key issues or ideas that the young person wants to talk about. This helps to build rapport between young people and adult interviewers, and can provide an extended understanding of young people's lives, language, perspectives and ideas. Unstructured interviews are most useful early in the participation process, providing the framework and necessary background information for developing a set of appropriate questions for subsequent structured and semi-structured interviews. However, they can also be useful later in the process as a way to gain a deeper and more thorough understanding of key issues. 'Guided tours' (page 127) are one form of unstructured interview that are useful later in the process as a follow-up to a structured or semi-structured interview.

Using aerial photos, maps and photographs of nearby places

Several Growing Up in Cities sites supplemented their interview questions with aerial photographs, maps and/or photographs of nearby places. In Melbourne, Australia, young people were asked to trace their range of movement through their local area on aerial photos, providing a basis for talking about where they go, how they get there, and why. In Oakland, USA, children were shown photographs of city landmarks and locations in a 1 mile (1.6 km) radius of the project site, and asked to identify the places and say whether they had been there. If they had, they were then asked to describe how often they went there, with whom, and what they did there. In another Oakland site, undertaken by students in a University of California-Berkeley planning studio, young people in the neighbourhood used a map of the local area to identify the places they went regularly, places they avoided, and the routes they traveled on a regular basis. The same mapped information was subsequently used for discussions about the local environment and how the neighbourhood could be improved.

© AIRCRAFT OPERATING COMPANY, JOHANNESBURG

Community residents, young and old, are intrigued by aerial photographs of their local area. Maps and aerial photographs — such as this one from the Johannesburg, South Africa GUIC site — can be used in interviews and small group discussions about the local area.

Developing an interview instrument

A successful interview requires a well-structured, clear and concise instrument. It should take participants through a logical sequence of questions that encourages reflection about their local area and their lives.

1. **Define the general topics to cover and develop draft questions.** Prepare a list of the general topics you would like to cover in the interviews, with a rough draft of the questions to ask under each topic category. Review the 'Sample topics and questions' on pages 110–111 for ideas, adding other topics and questions as needed. Once you have a complete list, review it to develop a logical sequence and remove redundancy. Consider how gender, race, ethnicity or religious issues might affect the interview, and whether it will be important to provide additional questions, or different wordings of questions, to understand issues specific to boys or girls or to particular groups.

2. **Start with 'easy' questions.** Start the interview with questions that are easy to answer, such as where they live and how long they have lived there. Beginning the interview with an exercise such as drawing (see page 115) can also be effective to help young participants to feel comfortable and provide a less formal basis for beginning the discussion.

3. **Refine the wording.** Be sensitive to the different meanings and connotations that words have for different groups, avoiding language that might be vague or misunderstood. Also, present potentially contentious or personal issues in a sensitive manner. The participation of young people from the local area in developing or reviewing the interview instrument can help to avoid problematic questions.

4. **Check the length.** Time the interview to make sure that it does not become too long or tiring for either the child or the interviewer. If it will take longer than 30 to 45 minutes, either remove questions or divide the interview into two sessions.

5. **Translate as necessary.** If multiple languages are spoken at your site, translate the questions into each language, being careful not to change the meaning of the questions in the translation process. Involve a professional translator if necessary.

6. **Format the instrument.** Format the instrument so that questions are easy to read and there is adequate space for taking notes during the interview. Longer questions should have just one question per page, while shorter, related questions may be grouped on a single page. It may also be appropriate or necessary to include notes to interviewers on the instrument itself. Include a reference number in the upper corner of the instrument (on every page) to facilitate coding and filing and to protect confidentiality. See the illustration on page 110 for an example of a formatted interview instrument.

7. **Pre-test and revise.** Once a formatted draft of the instrument is complete, pre-test it and revise accordingly before beginning the actual interviews.

Interviews

SAMPLE INTERVIEW TOPICS AND QUESTIONS

Identification
- Name
- Age
- Address
- Telephone (where applicable)

Residential history
- How long have you lived in the area?
- Did you live somewhere else before? Where?
- Can you locate your house or apartment on this map?

General perceptions
- How would you describe the area where you live to someone who had never been there before?

Place knowledge and use
- Please tell me all the places you know in your area. *(Keep a list of places and, if possible, identify the places on a map.)*
- In which of these places do you usually spend your time?
- What do you do there? *(Probe for specific activities, not just generalities such as 'play'.)*
- What is the furthest place where you have been in the city?

Favourite places / special places
- Which of the places that you listed is most important to you? Why is it important?
- Which is your favourite place? Why?
- When you are feeling bad, where do you go to feel better?

Problem places
- Are there places where you do not like to go? What do you dislike about these places?
- Are there places where you are not allowed to go? Who forbids you? What are their reasons?
- Are there places that you cannot get into? Do you wish you could?
- Are there dangerous places in your area? What makes them dangerous?

Child's Name / Ref #: _____

Date: _____

Special Places

9.   Whic~

~e discussed are most important to

~to help me know what

Child's Name / Ref #: _____   Date: _____

INTERVIEW 1

Preparation
- Arrange for a place to work where there will be minimal interruptions and distractions.
- Begin by introducing yourself, explaining that you are trying to find out how young people use the place where they live and what they think about it, and getting the child's permission to proceed with the interviews.

Identification

1.   Record the following information:

Name _____

Age

Place ownership

- Do you help to take care of any part of your area? What do you do there?
- Are there any places that feel like your own?
- Are there places where you feel like an outsider?
- Who owns the streets here? Who takes care of them?
- Are there any places that nobody owns?

Place changes

- Has the area where you live changed in your memory?
- Has it become better or worse? Why?
- If you could make changes to your place, what would they be?

Support network

- I would like to know about the people in your family and where they live. Who lives in your home? Do any other members of your family live in the area?
- Who else do you visit on a regular basis for help, advice, or just to spend time together?

See 'Family and support networks', page 121.

Daily schedule

- Tell me about the things you did yesterday, including where you went, the people with whom you spent time.
- What time did you wake up? How did you spend your morning? What time did you leave the house? Where did you go?

See 'Daily activity schedules', page 118.

Work

- Do you work?
- Who do you work for and where?
- Describe the place where you work. What is it like and what do you do?
- How long have you been working there?
- How many hours a week do you work? Do you have a regular schedule?
- How often do you get paid? What do you do with the money you earn?
- What things do you like about your work, and what things do you dislike?

Leisure time

- What time during the day or week do you usually have as 'free time'?
- What are your favourite things to do during these times? Where do you do these things?
- Do you spend your free time with other people? If so, who?
- Where do you spend your school holidays? (This may not be relevant in some places, but in others it can be a good indicator of the child's socio-economic status.)

Education/school

- Do you attend school?
- Describe your school for me.
- What time does school start and what time does it finish? How many days a week do you go?
- How do you get to school? How long does it take you?
- What are your favourite school activities? What are your least favourite?
- What do you like best about your school? What do you like least?

The future

- If you could travel ten years into the future and see how the place where you live now had changed, what do you think it would be like?
- Ten years from now, where would you like to live?

Closing

- How do you feel about this interview?
- Is there anything else that I should have asked?
- Do you have any suggestions about how this information could be used?

Interviews

Being an effective interviewer

- **Be prepared.** Be familiar with the interview questions, and be prepared with potential follow-up questions. Have a sense of how much time will be needed for each part of the interview, and try to keep it on schedule to get through all the questions in the time allotted.

© MELINDA SWIFT

Conduct interviews in a place where young people are comfortable and at ease, and sit on the same level as them.

- **Create a friendly, comfortable atmosphere.** Establish a friendly, informal tone at the beginning of the interview. Meet with young people in a place where they are comfortable and at ease, and sit on the same level as them. Devote adequate time and energy to building rapport with local young people before beginning the interview process.

- **Be sensitive to cultural norms.** Be sensitive to cultural norms for beginning, carrying out and ending a conversation (which may vary by age, gender or social status) and discussing (or not discussing) potentially contentious or personal issues. The participation of young people from the local area in the development or review of the instrument can help to avoid problematic interview questions and sensitize project staff members to local norms and expectations.

- **Be sensitive to gender, race, ethnicity and religion.** Children need to feel comfortable with the person they are talking to. This may mean that it is important that male team members interview boys and female team members interview girls (although this is certainly not always the case). Similarly, children from a racial, ethnic or religious minority may feel uncomfortable and guarded if interviewed by a project team member from the dominant group. Although these issues vary by culture, they are present in one form or another in every culture. They should be considered and responded to according to the needs and preferences of each child.

- **Do not gang up.** Have only one interviewer present and one young person. For small-group interaction methods, see page 147.

- **Take good notes.** Take complete, accurate and comprehensible notes. Develop a shorthand style of note-taking if possible. Immediately after each interview, review, organize and expand the interview notes. If it is not possible to tape the interviews, then take detailed, careful notes that capture both the substance and flavour of the interview. Strive to capture comments using young people's own words.

- **Be attentive.** Take note of body language and other cues that might give insights on the young person's attitudes or perspectives. The tone of their response can be as informative as what they say. Are they enthusiastic about the interview, or apathetic? Does their demeanour change over the course of the interview? Do they speak more forcefully at times, and less so at others? Do they tend to dwell on some topics, and want to skip others?

- **Be systematic.** The difference between a structured interview and an informal discussion is that everyone is asked the same questions, in the same way, in the same order. In this way, answers can be compared between different individuals and groups. If questions are asked differently or in a different order, it becomes difficult to draw conclusions from the comparison of answers.

- **Avoid leading questions.** A leading question is one that presumes the answer or leads the person being interviewed to answer in a certain way. For example, 'Do you think this is a dirty place?' or 'Do you like the beautiful park across the street?' Avoid using value-laden terms in the interview questions, and try to phrase questions to allow open-ended responses. For example, 'What words would you use to describe this place?' or 'Tell me about the park across the street. What kinds of things do you do there? What do you like about it? What do you not like about it?'

- **Ask follow-up questions.** If answers come up that might lead to valuable information, follow up with additional questions to request more details. Also, if initial answers to questions are vague or general, follow up by asking for more specifics. For example, if the answer is 'We go to the park a lot', follow up by asking 'How much is "a lot"? Can you be more specific?'

- **Guard against reactivity.** Reactivity refers to the ways in which people change their 'normal' behaviour in the presence of an outsider. For young people (and adults too), the novelty of taking part in a participatory project may be very stimulating, possibly leading them to neglect their other daily activities. They may respond by denigrating their usual activities, referring to them as 'boring' when they otherwise might not think of them as such. To overcome problems of reactivity, it is important to avoid leading questions; give consistent feedback (do not praise them for some answers and not for others); offer confidentiality; and never abuse trust.

Interviews

Interviews with parents, officials and other adults

(Questions adapted from Kevin Lynch, 1977)[2]

Interviews are also a useful tool for exploring the attitudes and insights of parents, community leaders, government officials, and other adults who affect children's lives. In general, many of the topics and questions listed here would apply to these groups as well. Other questions to consider include:

> What part of the day or night does your child normally spend outside the home? In what places and at what hours? What does he or she do there? How often do you see him/her?

> What did your child do yesterday, and where?

> Are those places suitable for what he or she was doing? If not, how should those places be changed?

> Is any of this activity unsafe, or improper, or wasteful? Why? How would you prefer your child's time be spent? What could be done about it?

> How much of the city does your child know, and how far does he or she go either alone or with friends?

> Where in the city do you take your child? Why? How often?

> What does your child need most? What do you need in order to take care of your child?

> How do you think your children's children will spend their time, and what will the places they live in be like? What do you wish those places could be?

© GUIC AUSTRALIA / L. HASLUCK

Interviews with older residents can help give insight regarding the community's history as well as the attitudes and perspectives of adults about the young people in their area.

> Tell me about what it was like when you were a child. What do you remember of the place you lived in, and what did you do there? How does that compare with the place your child is growing up in today? Which place was better to grow up in and why?

For officials, questions should explore their own perceptions of the area, including their evaluation of it as a place for young people, and their knowledge about young people's use of the area, their activities, and what they like most and least about the area. Questions could also explore officials' own memories of their childhood environment and comparisons with the project area environment. Lastly, and importantly, officials should be questioned about their plans for the area; how they believe their plans will affect the quality of the area and, specifically, the quality of young people's lives; what types of data and criteria they typically rely on in the development of their plans; and how young people in the area and other community residents can be involved in the planning process.

METHOD

Drawings

© ROBIN MOORE

Young people's drawings of their local area provide a tool for discussing their perceptions of the area, their activities, their range of movement, and their favourite and least favourite places. Observations of the drawing process and the drawings themselves can provide insights about what is most and least important to young people. Drawings can be integrated as part of the one-to-one interviews, or done as a separate activity. They are a very engaging information-gathering technique and as such are a good 'ice-breaker' activity for early in the process. They also provide a good starting point for conducting interviews and for launching exercises such as guided tours.

PHOTO LEFT: Making a drawing of the local area provides a good starting point for interviews and for sharing information about activities, range of movement and favourite/least favourite places.

PURPOSE

> Engage young people in a fun and creative activity.
> Initiate discussions on various aspects of the local area.
> Provide a tool for analysing what young people value about their environment.
> Develop a visual database of young people's perspectives on their local area.

TIME REQUIRED

Drawings require very little preparation time other than organizing the materials and arranging a time and place. The drawing process may take anywhere from 5 to 30 minutes per participant, with the discussion of the drawing taking another 10 to 15 minutes each. However, do not make it a 'timed' activity: it is not a race, nor is it an art contest. Give participants as much time as they need, and provide additional sheets of paper if necessary so they can extend the area they depict. Doing the drawings in small groups can save time, though discussion of the drawings should ideally be done one-to-one, especially with younger children.

Drawings

FINE POINT PEN

MEDIUM POINT PEN

HEAVY POINT PEN

Fine point pens make lines that are too thin to photocopy, while pens that are too thick make it difficult to draw.

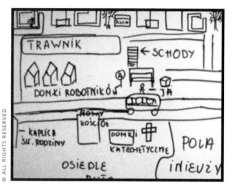

The drawing of a twelve-year-old Polish boy shows the area where he lives.

MATERIALS NEEDED

> Large sheets of good-quality, durable paper. A2 (420x594 mm) or tabloid (11x17 inches) sheets work well. Plan for at least two sheets per participant.
> Black, medium-point water-based marking pens
> Wax crayons for adding colour (do not use yellow, which is difficult to read)
> Pencil for adding notes
> Notepad and pen/pencil for taking notes

MAXIMIZING YOUNG PEOPLE'S PARTICIPATION

> *Give a complete explanation of the exercise.* Explain clearly why participants are being asked to do a drawing and how their input will be used.
> *Show respect and sensitivity.* Respect young people's right not to participate and be sensitive to the issues that the drawing exercise might raise, such as evoking painful memories or leading to feelings of inadequacy or embarrassment.
> *Do not interrupt.* Do not comment or interrupt while they are drawing.
> *Provide enough time.* Provide adequate time for all participants to draw and then to explain or interpret their drawings.
> *Acknowledge that participants own their drawings.* Ask their permission to use, keep, display or publish their drawings, and give them a copy if they request one. Ask if they want their names to be given with their drawings.
> *Give equal value to all drawings.* Make sure that participants understand that there are no 'good' or 'bad' drawings. All of them are valuable.

PROCESS GUIDE

1. **Explain the exercise.** Start with a general question, such as:

   'Would you please make a drawing of the area around where you live, so that you can show me the places where you go and the places that are important to you?'

   Remember, the drawing does not need to be a map, although you should encourage participants to focus on outdoor public and semi-public places.

2. **Take notes.** While the drawing is being made, take careful notes about what is drawn first, second, third; how the pieces are put together; where the edges of the territory are defined; what places are most emphasized; and areas that seem confused.

3. **Provide additional sheets.** Provide extra paper as necessary to extend or enlarge the drawing. Attach extra sheets with tape on the back of the paper.

4. **Discuss the drawing.** Once the drawing is developed, ask probing follow-up questions to clarify what the drawing contains and elicit more detailed information, such as the types of activity they associate with each place and their feelings for it. Focus on their perception of the environment (what is important to them and why) and on outdoor, public or semi-public spaces. Remember that the discussion that develops around the drawing is the most important part of this exercise — not the drawing itself.

5. **Make notations on the drawing.** Ask each participant to label the main features of the drawing to make the content clear. Or ask if it would be all right for you to write on the drawing, making light pencil notes only.

© DAVID DRISKELL

6. **Label the drawing.** On the back of the paper, ask each participant to write his or her name, age, date, address, and telephone number if there is one. Also record their gender.

7. **Copy and store the drawing.** Ask if you can keep the picture. If they would prefer to keep the original, ask if you can make a copy for yourself. Make sure all drawings are properly filed and stored (see page 94), and do not change or 'improve' anything on the original drawing.

Drawings provide a basis for discussing young people's perceptions of the local environment as well as information about where they go and what they do. The discussion about the drawing is the most important part of the exercise.

Drawing in small groups

Drawing in small groups of four or five can create an atmosphere in which young people feel less inhibited. Be sure to provide enough space so that everyone can be comfortable and able to work without disruption from others. On the same day or the following day, do one-to-one follow-up interviews to discuss and annotate each drawing. The follow-up interviews will probably take between 10 and 15 minutes each, unless the drawing is being used as the first step in a lengthier interview. In this case it may not be possible to do drawings in small groups, unless there are enough team members to conduct all the interviews within one day of the drawing exercise.

The drawing exercise can also be used as the introduction to a focus group session, with participants displaying and comparing their drawings. See 'Focus groups and small-group discussions', page 147.

METHOD

Daily Activity Schedules

Understanding the activities that young people engage in during a typical day and the ways that they use their free time can provide valuable insights into their lives and values, including the ways in which they use the local area. The daily activity schedule is a simple technique for documenting time use. Rather than asking for general estimates of how much time is typically spent on various activities, it asks young people to provide a detailed account of the activities they undertook on a specific day that is fresh in their memory (usually the day before). The difficult part of this activity is that young people's daily schedules change significantly depending on the season, whether or not they are attending school that day, whether it is a weekday or weekend, and whether it is a public holiday, religious festival, or other special event.

Activity schedule forms should be designed so that they are easy to understand and fill out. The exact format may vary based on the age and experience of participants. Be sure to include both the date the form was filled out and the day on which the recorded activities took place.

PURPOSE

> Document young people's activities over the course of a day.

> Document where young people go and whom they see.

> Compare young people's statements about their lives with a more systematic documentation of how and where they spend their time.

TIME REQUIRED

Daily activity schedules require very little preparation time other than organizing the materials. The process of filling out an activity schedule with a young person or reviewing a schedule with them that they have filled in on their own may take between 15 to 30 minutes.

MATERIALS NEEDED

> Activity schedule forms on which to record times and activities

> Pencils

Interviewer D. BROWN
Date Completed 2-1-01
CHILD'S NAME: RASHEED
Ref. # BOY 03
DATE (for which the schedule has been completed): TUESDAY, JANUARY 27 (SCHOOL DAY)

Please describe what you did yesterday, beginning with when you woke up in the morning, and ending with when you went to sleep at night. Describe not only what you did, but where you were and who was with you.

6:00 AM

6:30 AM   6:45 — WOKE UP
7:00 AM   — CHANGED CLOTHES — WASHED FACE + MADE BED
7:30 AM   BREAKFAST (w/ SISTER + MOM)
           — WASHED DISHES
8:00 AM   FINISHED HOMEWORK
           8:05 — TOOK SCHOOL BUS
8:30 AM   8:15 — AT SCHOOL / PLAYED w/ FRIENDS OUTSIDE IN GRASS AREA
           8:30 — SCHOOL STARTS
9:00 AM
           MATH (EXAM)
9:30 AM
10:00 AM
           ENGLISH
10:30 AM   PRESENTATION.
11:00 AM   GYM CLASS
11:30 AM   11:45 LUNCH BREAK
12:00 PM (noon)

MAXIMIZING YOUNG PEOPLE'S PARTICIPATION

> *Give a complete explanation of the exercise.* Explain clearly why participants are being asked to document their daily schedule and how the information will be used.

> *Show respect and sensitivity.* Respect young people's right not to participate and be sensitive to personal and cultural issues about privacy. It may be inappropriate to probe about some activities, especially activities within the family or home environment. Also, young people may be hesitant to talk about painful issues in their lives or may feel inadequate or embarrassed if they are unable to tell time or to recall their activities with complete accuracy.

> *Provide enough time.* Provide adequate time for participants to think about, develop and discuss their activity schedules.

> *Do not judge.* Do not give your own opinions about the relative value of some activities over others.

PROCESS GUIDE

1. **Define your approach.** To complete an activity schedule, young people must identify the beginning and end times for each activity, noting where the activity took place and who else was involved. For younger participants, it will be easiest for a project staff member to sit down with them to review their memory of what they did the day before, filling in a simplified activity schedule. Older participants can be given a blank (and more detailed) activity schedule to fill in on their own or to take with them and fill in over the course of a day, subsequently discussing their completed schedule with a member of the team.

2. **Prepare an activity schedule form.** Develop a form that fits your project's needs. For younger participants, use a form with larger time blocks or with 'times' that are related to fixed daily events (e.g. 'before breakfast' or 'before school'). For older participants, consider dividing the time schedule into smaller (15 minute) time segments.

3. **Determine which days to conduct the exercise.** It is important that the day on which you will meet to conduct the exercise should be carefully selected, as participants will be asked to either describe the day immediately preceding or to take the activity schedule with them and fill it out on the day immediately following. Avoid times when young people's schedules will be different to usual (such as during a religious or national holiday).

   Consider how you can best collect information for both weekday schedules and weekend schedules, as there are significant differences between them. Ideally, each young person would complete an activity schedule for both a weekday and a weekend.

This may be difficult, however, given time constraints. Consider documenting weekday activities in an interview format with each participant, and then having them take an additional form to fill in over a weekend. Alternatively, divide participants so that some of them complete their schedules for weekdays and others for weekends (but be careful not to skew the data inadvertently; for example, by having only girls or only older children do weekend schedules).

Clock faces and timelines

The South African GUIC team developed a variation on the daily activity schedule in which young people were asked to draw clocks on large sheets of paper (a large circle with numbers around it, creating a large clock face). They were then asked to draw the activities alongside the clock face, showing what they did the day before at different hours. The team member then discussed the drawing with each child to elicit more specific information about the activity and its duration. The format was found to be much more approachable, although it tended to deliver less precise results.

The Norwegian GUIC team used another variation, recording activities on a linear 'timeline' chart, providing an approachable and interactive format, and reflecting the fact that many of the children were used to telling time from a digital clock rather than from a traditional analogue clock face.

4. **Explain the exercise.** Explain to each participant the purpose of the exercise and how the information will be used. Give instructions for filling out the activity schedule to older children who want to take it with them and fill it in the next day. Encourage them to carry the schedule with them, periodically making notes about their activities and spending some time at the end of the day filling in additional details.

5. **Complete the activity schedule.** For children who fill in the schedule with a project staff member, begin with the time that they woke up the day before and work through their activities during each part of the day. Try to be as specific as possible about the times that different activities started and ended, but if they cannot remember the exact time, an approximate time will do. For children who do not track their day according to a clock, the time spent in each activity must be keyed to specific events during the day (e.g. before school, after lunch, before sunset, etc.). The results in this case will provide a sense of the sequence of activities and the relative amount of time spent. In any case, fill in details as much as possible — where were they during each part of the day and who was with them.

6. **Review the completed schedules.** For young people who fill in their own schedule over the course of a day, spend time reviewing their completed schedule with them. Try to meet with them on the day immediately following the day they filled it out, so that details are fresh in their memory. Through the discussion, try to complete any missing details and check for any inconsistencies that might reflect confusion in how to fill in the form.

Be sure that each completed schedule is properly coded with the participant's name, reference number or alias (see note on 'Confidentiality' on page 92).

METHOD

Family and Support Networks[3]

Family networks often play an extremely significant role in young people's lives, and can be supplemented (or sometimes replaced) by support networks of neighbours and friends. It is important to understand this vital social dimension of young people's lives, and how it affects their self-image, quality of life, and experience of place. Through this one-to-one activity, participants document and talk about their family and support networks. The method can be incorporated into an interview or done as a separate exercise.

PURPOSE

> Document family and social-support networks.
> Understand social-support relationships and dynamics.
> Understand the importance of non-family adults, such as neighbours and close friends.
> Understand how family and support networks affect young people's quality of life and sense of place.

TIME REQUIRED

This activity requires very little preparation time other than organizing the materials and scheduling one-to-one time with the participants. Approximately 15 to 30 minutes are required to conduct the exercise with each young person.

MATERIALS NEEDED

> Paper (larger sheets work best)
> Markers (several colours)
> Scissors and glue or tape (optional)

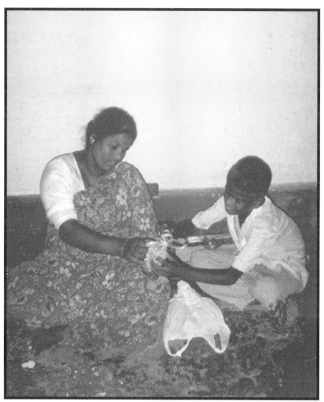

Understanding young people's relationships with family and friends is essential for understanding their experiences and perspectives.

MAXIMIZING YOUNG PEOPLE'S PARTICIPATION

> *Give a complete explanation of the exercise.* Explain clearly to the participants the purpose of the activity and how the information will be used.

> *Show respect and sensitivity.* Respect young people's right not to participate and be sensitive to personal and cultural issues about privacy that may cause some young people to feel uncomfortable talking about their family and other close relationships. Be especially sensitive to painful issues this exercise might raise, such as why some children have only one or no parents, while others have both a mother and father. This can be particularly distressing in places where children have lost family members due to war, displacement or disease. In such instances a less direct form of exploring family relations and support networks may be warranted (for example through role-play or puppetry; see page 124).

> *Provide enough time.* Provide adequate time for participants to think about, develop and discuss their family and support networks.

> *Do not judge.* Avoid voicing your opinions about the closeness or quality of their family network and other adult relationships.

PROCESS GUIDE

1. **Explain the exercise.** After explaining the purpose of the exercise, give basic instructions to the young person with whom you are working, for example:

   We are going to make a picture showing all the people in your family — parents, brothers and sisters, grandparents, cousins, aunts, uncles and so on. We will use triangles for the men and boys, and circles for the women and girls. We will start in the middle with you and the people who live with you in your house.

2. **Develop the family network diagram.** Work with the young person to begin the family network diagram, then watch it grow. Use consistent symbols to denote males and females and draw circles around groups of people who live together. Note on the diagram where each group lives and, if possible, approximate ages of the children. If the participant does not know exactly how old all his or her cousins are, simply note their general age (infant, toddler, young child, adolescent, young adult).

3. **Extend the diagram to include other important relations.** Ask the young person to also identify people in his/her life who are like family, even if they are not related by blood. This may include neighbours or friends who are involved in their care, either through formal or informal arrangements. Provide distinct symbols to denote these people, and place them on the diagram based on their physical proximity to the child's home. Differentiate the linkages between the child and these individuals from the linkages between the child and his or her family.

4. **Discuss the final diagram.** Use the diagram to discuss the child's family relationships and social network. Sample questions to ask include:

How often do you see each of these people?

For the people you see regularly, how do you get to their house? What sorts of things do you do there? Do you go with your mother and father, or your brothers and sisters, or do you go by yourself?

Which of these people do you most like to visit? Why?

Which of them do you least like to visit? Why?

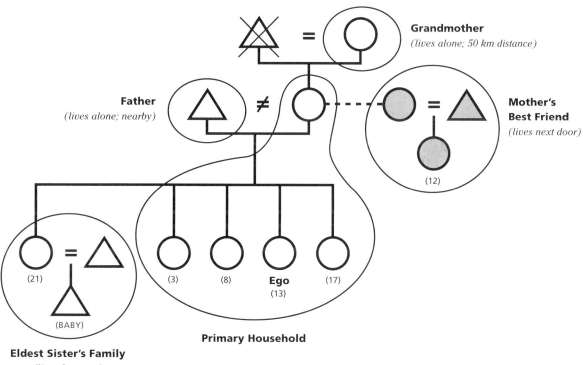

A sample diagram shows the family and social support network of a child (marked 'Ego' on the diagram). Circles denote females, triangles denote males. An 'equals' sign denotes marriage (=) or divorce (≠). Symbols with an 'X' through them denote people who are deceased. Ages of children are indicated in parentheses. Larger circles are drawn around household groupings, and greytone symbols and dotted lines indicate other relationships important to the child.

METHOD

Role-Play, Drama and Puppetry

© JILL SWART-KRUGER

A child at the South African GUIC site uses a dramatic replay to describe a personal incident as part of a facilitator-led small group discussion with other girls and boys.

Some young people find it easier to communicate through role-play, puppetry and other forms of drama rather than answer direct questions in an interview. Many cultures have a strong tradition of street theatre, puppetry and other forms of dramatic expression that may make it easier for young people to express their ideas and opinions indirectly, as the character is speaking rather than themselves. These methods are particularly useful for exploring sensitive issues and for finding out young people's views about adults. Role-play, drama and puppetry can be used in conjunction with small-group discussions or focus groups to stimulate discussion or to explore key issues. They are also useful early in the process as warm-up exercises and for initial explorations of young people's ideas and perspectives. Dramatic productions that are written, directed and acted by young people can also be an effective vehicle for communicating their issues to a larger audience.

PURPOSE

> Allow young people to communicate their ideas, opinions and perspectives in a non-threatening manner.
> Help to develop rapport among young people and with adult team members.
> Draw upon local forms of communication and storytelling.
> Communicate issues and ideas to a larger audience.

TIME REQUIRED

The time required for undertaking role-play, puppetry exercises and other dramatic forms will vary widely — from 15 to 30 minutes (for quick role-play exercises) to several months (for performances developed and produced by young people).

MATERIALS NEEDED

Materials will vary widely, from virtually nothing; to simple costumes, props or puppets; to elaborate stage sets. Project staff members should always have a notebook and pen or pencil to document the activities as they unfold, and a camera if young people agree to have photographs taken.

MAXIMIZING YOUNG PEOPLE'S PARTICIPATION

> *Give a complete explanation.* Explain clearly what participants are being asked to do, and why.

> *Show respect and sensitivity.* Be sensitive to personal and cultural issues that may cause some young people to feel uncomfortable in a 'performance'. Respect their right not to participate if they do not want to, and be sensitive to painful issues that might be raised.

> *Provide privacy.* Do not encourage a public audience unless young people request it.

> *Let young people lead.* Allow young people to select their own roles and to define the content of their role-play to the fullest extent possible. Older participants can take the lead in producing and directing their own performances, from defining a storyline to making costumes and sets.

> *Provide enough time.* Provide adequate time for children to develop their role-play and to reflect on and discuss it afterwards.

> *Do not judge.* Validate everyone's contributions and performances equally.

PROCESS GUIDE

The exact steps will vary based on the size of the group, form of expression, and time and resources available.

1. **Select and/or train team members appropriately.** It is important that all team members understand and appreciate the value of these methods, be skilled in setting them up and facilitating them, and be prepared to address the issues raised in a sensitive and thoughtful manner. Plays, puppetry and other forms of artistic expression provide excellent opportunities to involve community artists in the participation process. However, make sure that they are given an introduction to the project and its goals, and an orientation to working with young people in participatory ways.

2. **Define the subject and form of expression.** Facilitate a discussion with young people to determine what the purpose and subject of the role-play, puppet show or other dramatic form of expression will be. If such exercises are a new experience for young people, start with something simple and approachable (but stimulating), work-

Role-Play, Drama and Puppetry

ing in small groups. Draw upon forms of expression that are known to them or which are prevalent in the local culture.

3. **Encourage creativity.** Encourage everyone to participate, but respect the right not to participate for those who may be uncomfortable in a 'performance' situation. Work in small groups, emphasize the collaborative and playful nature of the activity, and de-emphasize the 'performance' aspect. Provide opportunities for everyone to participate to the extent that they desire, and encourage new forms of creative expression as participants become more familiar with improvization and can use it more effectively to explore issues and feelings.

Participants in a training workshop use role play to explore issues about adult-youth interactions in participatory projects.

4. **Facilitate reflection and discussion.** Creative forms of expression can communicate a range of ideas, perspectives, and feelings. All role-plays, puppet shows and other forms of dramatic expression need to be followed by small-group discussions to reflect on what was revealed through the exercise and what the group might learn from it. As many participants will find it easier to communicate their feelings through a role-play or similar method, facilitators must be prepared to deal with troubling or sensitive issues that may arise, and provide counselling support if necessary.

    At the end of the activity, reflect on what was effective about the method that was used, and what could have been done differently.

5. **Document the results.** As in all project activities, ensure that the methods used and their results are properly documented. Also note the group's evaluation of the method and how it could be improved in the future.

METHOD

Guided Tours

Tours that are guided by young people are consistently one of the most valuable methods for understanding their perspectives on and use of the local environment. Viewing places first-hand often elicits new information and serves as a catalyst for more in-depth questions and discussion. To be of most use, guided tours should come after some of the other activities (such as interviews and drawings) when young people have developed a stronger relationship of trust with project team members, and team members have some initial information on the places they will be seeing.

© ROBIN MOORE

In a variation on the child-led tour at the GUIC site in Buenos Aires, Argentina, the tour is joined by the child's mother, providing both child and parent perspectives on neighbourhood issues.

PURPOSE

> Visit places within the local area that are important to young people.
> Directly observe and photograph the places and issues that have been identified during other activities.
> Develop a better understanding of key issues in the local area and discuss them in greater depth.
> Understand the connections and routes between various places in the community, and how young people move through it.
> Interact with young people in the context of their local area.

TIME REQUIRED

Guided tours take time, requiring between 30 minutes to a couple of hours depending on the participant and the size of the area. If children know each other well, they can conduct the tours in pairs.

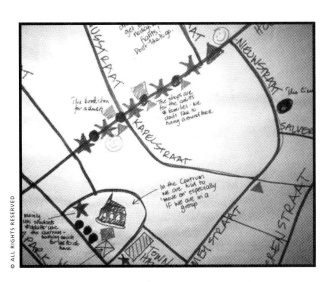

A map summarizes the input from a number of walking tours, highlighting favourite and least favourite places, activity centres, and other important neighbourhood features.

MATERIALS NEEDED

> Notebook
> Pen or pencil
> Camera and film or disks (optional — see 'Using a camera', page 102)

MAXIMIZING YOUNG PEOPLE'S PARTICIPATION

> *Give a complete explanation.* Explain the purpose of the walking tour and how the information that is collected will be used.

> *Show respect and sensitivity.* Be sensitive to young people's potential discomfort in conducting a 'walking tour' with adults who may be from outside the area, and respect their right not to participate if they do not want to.

> *Let them lead.* Allow young people to determine the places to be visited and the paths taken to get there (be prepared to climb over fences, jump over ditches, and speak with their friends and relatives). Do not insist on visiting a place where a young person does not want to go.

> *Allow enough time.* Provide adequate time to visit every place where they want to go and to discuss the places as much as they would like.

> *Do not judge.* Strive to understand how they perceive each area. Do not praise or denigrate any of the places, or communicate your own perceptions and biases.

PROCESS GUIDE

1. **Introduce this method late in the process.** Guided tours should only be conducted after project staff members have developed relationships of trust and respect with participants. This may take some time, but it is essential in order to make the guided tours worthwhile. For this reason, guided tours are usually conducted later in the evaluation process, as a follow-up to interviews or other activities.

2. **Introduce the exercise.** Explain to participants the purpose of the guided tours and how the information will be used. Ask them to give you a tour of the local area, showing you where they spend their time and describing when they go there, what they do there, who is there with them, and any issues they think are important about the place. Ask them to identify favourite places, dangerous places, problem places, special places, and other places that are significant to them or visited by them on a regular basis.

   Introduce the tour purpose and structure at least two days in advance so that they can give it some thought and plan a route of the places they want to show you. If possible, leave the amount of time open-ended so that it will not be rushed. But if time is limited, let all participants know the timeframe in advance.

3. **Take the tour.** Conduct guided tours either one-to-one or in pairs of good friends. During the tour, take notes (with their permission) of the route and the places they show you, capturing the main points of their description of each place. Ideally, have a photocopy of a local area map to mark the route and identify the places to which they take you. Also, ask permission to take photographs of the places you visit to provide a visual record of the tour.

4. **Compile notes.** When the tour is completed, thank all the participants for their time, energy and insights. Spend a few minutes immediately after the tour completing and organizing your notes to make sure that all the key points are documented and any map or photo annotations are properly recorded. As always, make sure that all notes and materials are properly organized and filed. A compilation of the notes can be used in small group discussions to further explore the issues raised in the guided tours.

Wheeling around

While most guided tours are conducted on foot, many young people move through the local area by bicycle, scooter, or skateboard, which changes where they go, and how far they travel. Young people at the GUIC site in Melbourne, Australia, conducted a guided tour by bicycle to show where they go and discuss issues in the local area.

Guided Tours

Photographs by Young People

Photography encourages young people to look at their local area in new ways and provides an opportunity to document their perspectives and ideas in a fun and creative manner.

© ROBIN MOORE

Photographs taken by young people can be a valuable tool for gathering information on their environmental perceptions and attitudes, enhancing information collected through the interviews and other methods. Photographs can become the basis for discussions about the local area as well as providing visual data about it. They are also effective for initiating communication with the larger community through gallery displays. However, photography should not be proposed if it is considered culturally inappropriate. In terms of camera equipment, inexpensive reloadable cameras are recommended as they do not cost more than 'disposable' cameras, are simple to use, can be used repeatedly, and are more environmentally friendly. If you can afford a digital camera, it can be an excellent tool for this type of activity. If the equipment is accessible, short videos made by young people can be similarly effective.

PURPOSE

> Engage young people in a fun and creative activity.
> Develop a visual database on young people's perspectives of their local area.
> Stimulate discussions on various aspects of the local area.
> Communicate young people's perspectives to the larger community.

TIME REQUIRED

Preparation time is required for purchasing cameras and film. The initial method introduction to participants takes about 15 minutes. The actual photo-taking process can vary from several hours to a week or more, depending on the age group, the size of the area and how the exercise is structured. Once the film is processed, young people should meet to discuss the photographs and write captions. Additional time will be needed to organize and present them as a 'gallery' exhibit or album that can be shared with others.

MATERIALS NEEDED

> Camera(s) (inexpensive, reusable, cameras work well — flash is recommended to allow for indoor and night-time photographs)
> Extra batteries
> Film (or disks, if digital camera). Use colour print film because prints are much easier to share and discuss. 200 ISO film is recommended as it can be used both indoors and outdoors.

MAXIMIZING YOUNG PEOPLE'S PARTICIPATION

> *Give a complete explanation.* Explain the purpose of taking photographs and how they will be used.
> *Show respect and sensitivity.* Be sensitive to young people's potential discomfort in taking photographs in the community, and respect their right not to participate if they do not want to. Also, be considerate of the economic value and potential novelty of a camera. Even a simple box camera may cost more than some households' monthly income. Be sensitive to the issues this may raise.
> *Give clear operating instructions.* Carefully explain how to use the camera, including how to load and unload the film, how to operate the shutter, and how to advance the film. Let participants practice before loading the film into the camera. If the camera has a flash or other features, explain how to use those as well.
> *Let them lead.* Allow young people to determine what they photograph and how.
> *Provide enough time.* Provide adequate time for taking the photographs and for explaining each photograph once they are developed.
> *Acknowledge that young people own their photographs.* Ask their permission to use, keep, display or publish their photographs, giving them an extra copy of each if they request one. Ask if they want their name to be given with their photographs.
> *Do not judge.* There are no 'good' or 'bad' photographs. They each have a story to tell. If only some are to be selected for display, ask the child who shot the photographs to make the selection.

Photographs by Young People

PROCESS GUIDE

1. **Introduce the exercise.** Explain to the participants that they will each be given a turn with a camera and asked to photograph things in their local area. Ask them to photograph places that are important to them, places with problems, or other aspects of their environment that they would like to communicate to others.

2. **Explain how to operate the camera.** Give participants a camera, film, and very basic instruction on how to operate the camera. If using a digital camera, explain clearly how to take the photographs and make sure everyone has a disk with their name clearly marked on it. Giving detailed instructions in photography will interfere with their creative process. Simply give them the camera and film, show them the camera's basic operation, and make sure the film or disk is loaded properly.

   If you have limited resources, participants can rotate turns on a few cameras, each taking a limited number of photographs (rationed based on how much film and developing you can afford and the number of participants).

An informal display of young people's photographs provides opportunities for discussion with adults and other community members at a workshop in Haarlem, the Netherlands.

© DAVID DRISKELL

3. **Take photographs.** Agree upon a day when the cameras and film or disks will be returned for processing. Allow about a week for the young people to visit all the places they would like to photograph. Alternatively, if the activity must be completed the same day, establish a meeting time and place, allowing adequate time for completing the activity (at least several hours).

4. **Develop, review and caption the photographs.** Once all participants have finished shooting photographs, have them return the film to the project team for processing (or printing, if using digital cameras). When the photographs are ready, meet with each participant (or, if the camera was shared, the participants who shared it) to review the photographs, what they contain, and why they were taken. Include notes on the approximate date, time and location of each, as well as on the subject matter.

   If the resources are available, make an extra copy of each photograph for the young people to keep. If not, ask their permission to keep the photographs, giving them the option of selecting any that they would like to keep.

Photographs by Young People

5. **Develop a gallery exhibit or photograph album.** Ask participants if they would like to organize a community exhibition of their photographs. If so, help them to prepare gallery displays or an album that will facilitate viewing by others while protecting their work. Ask each participant to choose the photographs that they would like to include in the exhibit or album, and ask them to write a caption for each.

6. **Catalogue and store the photographs, negatives and notes.** Catalogue and store both negatives and prints in a safe location. Ideally, store them in plastic sleeves in three-ring binders to ensure that they do not become scratched, dusty or (worst of all) lost. If the images are being stored digitally, make sure that the disk is clearly labelled and backed up in a safe place. Also, make sure that the captions or notes are keyed to each photograph and stored. In the notes or captions, include names of people in the photo (as much as possible), place, date/time and name of photographer.

'Our neighbourhood is like that!'

Young people participating in the Growing Up in Cities project in the Boca-Barracas neighbourhood of Buenos Aires, Argentina, developed an exhibition of their photographs to express their perceptions and ideas to the larger community. The process of developing the exhibition involved three design workshops with a self-selected subgroup of children. They decided on a title for the exhibition ('Boca Barracas: Our Neighbourhood Is Like That!'), developed an exhibition catalogue, and invented slogans to promote the exhibition. The exhibition was the inaugural show for the grand opening of the new La Boca Popular Library during the Winter Vacation Festival at La Boca in 1997.

© NILDA COSCO

Photographs by Young People

METHOD

Behaviour Mapping

Behaviour mapping is a systematic observation technique for documenting the use of a specific space or location. It is not an explicitly participatory method, although it can be easily transformed into one, involving young people in the process of understanding and documenting how a space is used. Behaviour mapping is most useful relatively late in the evaluation process, after specific locations within the local area have been identified as being problematic, successful, or as presenting opportunities for redesign or reuse. It is a time-intensive exercise in which the activities observed within a defined area are noted on a map, with detail about the activities captured through map symbols, notes and photographs. The aim is to document how the space is being used, or not used, and the reasons

Participants at a training workshop in Bangalore, India, practice their behaviour-mapping skills in a local park.

that may lie behind those patterns of use (for example, seating is used when it is in the shade, but not when in full sun; or a play area near a school is used by young children on weekdays, and as a teen hangout on weekends). This provides information to confirm findings from other methods (such as interviews or guided tours), and can be particularly useful for determining appropriate site interventions, such as redesign of a plaza, reconfiguration of a pedestrian crossing, or reprogramming of uses in public buildings or outdoor spaces.

© DAVID DRISKELL

PURPOSE

> Document use of specific place.

> Identify physical characteristics of a place that shape its use, either negatively or positively.

> Identify factors in a specific space that might account for differences in use by age, gender or ethnic group.

> Confirm or clarify issues about a specific location that young people have raised through interviews, guided tours and other methods.

TIME REQUIRED

Preparation time is required to develop a base map and mapping symbols and to conduct staff training. The actual mapping is typically conducted over the course of several weeks, at various times of day and on various days of the week. It may also be necessary to conduct mapping at various times of the year (summer versus winter; school session versus school break). Alternatively, if the need is to compare the use of different parts of a space during peak times (on a summer weekend for example), it may be sufficient to conduct the study during a more limited period.

MATERIALS NEEDED

> Base map (see Item 3 of the 'Process guide')

> Pen or pencil

> Clipboard or other writing surface

> Camera and film or disks (optional, but recommended — see 'Using a camera', page 102)

MAXIMIZING YOUNG PEOPLE'S PARTICIPATION

> *Give a complete explanation.* Explain the purpose of behaviour mapping and how the information will be used.

> *Let young people decide.* Let young people identify the areas to be mapped and decide whether 'behaviour mapping' is an appropriate method to use.

> *Involve young people in the mapping.* Have young people, especially older youth, help to conduct the study, providing training for those who are interested.

PROCESS GUIDE

1. **Begin behaviour mapping after initial data collection.** Behaviour mapping is typically most useful when conducted after initial data-collection activities have taken place, when there is a stronger sense about what the key locations are that need to be better understood. This initial information may be gained through methods such as 'Interviews' (page 103), 'Guided tours' (page 127), and 'Photographs by young people' (page 130).

2. **Focus on key places and/or key issues.** Select places within the local area that were identified through the participatory evaluation activities as being particularly important or problematic. These may include official community-defined spaces (such as a public square or play area) as well as informal spaces defined by young people themselves (such as a hangout space or vacant lot).

Behaviour Mapping

For the purpose of behaviour mapping, it is easiest if the places have well-defined boundaries and are small enough to be observed from one or two vantage points. Places that are good candidates for behaviour mapping include streets or paths, hangout places, gardens, playgrounds, eating places, workplaces, and similar locations where young people regularly engage in a particular type of activity. You may also want to consider those areas where young people do not go because they may feel unwelcome or uncomfortable, or consider focusing on particular issues or activities that have been identified as concerns. For example, the number of cars that fail to stop at an intersection, or the number of people who drop litter in a public place.

3. **Prepare a base map for each location.** Prepare a base map of the specific location where you will be documenting activities. This can be a hand-drawn map, drawn roughly to scale and large enough to accommodate the mapping symbols. Include all the physical details on the base map that might affect behaviour (such as benches, walls, trees, utility poles, level changes, raised planting beds, fences). Omit details that do not affect how people use the space.

4. **Map the space at different times of the day, on different days of the week or weekend.** Map activities at the site at two or three different times on a single day, and on a couple of different days of the week, including weekends. Choose times when the area will have high levels of use, and times when there will be fewer people or different types of user. Brief preliminary visits to the site at various times will help to identify the most appropriate times to conduct the mapping.

5. **Note the time of day, date and weather.** Note the date and time of day for each round of mapping. Also note the local weather conditions at the time (temperature, wind strength and direction, precipitation, level of light, noise).

6. **Plot the users.** The purpose of the mapping is to record, as quickly and systematically as possible, the location and movement of users at the site, and the activities of different types of user. Use a consistent set of symbols to differentiate between different types of user and types of activity. A basic set of mapping symbols is shown in the example on page 138.

7. **Add notes and photographs.** Supplement the map symbols with notes and photographs to record more detail. Use photographs to record visual information such as people's dress and the general location of activities in relation to major site features. Make notes about motion, details of behaviour, speech (where possible), and how people use (or do not use) the spatial features around them. If necessary, ask questions of people within the space to fully understand their activities and behaviours.

8. **Key observations and photos to the map.** Key the locations of photographs and specific notes to the map.

9. **Document the volume of people moving through the site.** It can be very difficult to map the number of pedestrians, cyclists or others who move through the site along major paths of travel. For these situations, note on the map the major paths of travel and simply count the number of people or bikes that move along each path over a five minute period, using photographs and notes to supplement. Are there features in the environment that direct the path of travel or affect pedestrian behaviour?

10. **Conduct as many 'cycles' of mapping as necessary until the patterns of behaviour and use are clear.** Each mapping session will probably take up to an hour before the map becomes too difficult to read. Larger areas may require more time and more people, with multiple teams simultaneously mapping different parts of the site. Revisit the site at different times of day and on different days of the week until the patterns of activity and behaviour become obvious and you have ample documentation.

11. **Organize and archive the results.** Properly organize and file completed map diagrams, notes and photos after each mapping cycle.

12. **Analyse and discuss the results.** Compile the plots of each cycle of behaviour on a single master map that can be used in a small group discussion to compare and contrast the various patterns that emerge. What parts of the space are most used? What parts are used very little, or not at all? What factors seem to be shaping these patterns of use? Do these patterns confirm information that was gathered through other methods? What lessons are there in terms of possible redesign or reuse of the space? Are there things that could be done to make the space more usable to a wider range of people, or at different times of the day or week? Are there ways to improve the use of those parts of the space that are not currently being used? What parts of the space are working well, and what should be done to ensure that they continue to work well?

Behaviour Mapping

A behaviour mapping diagram

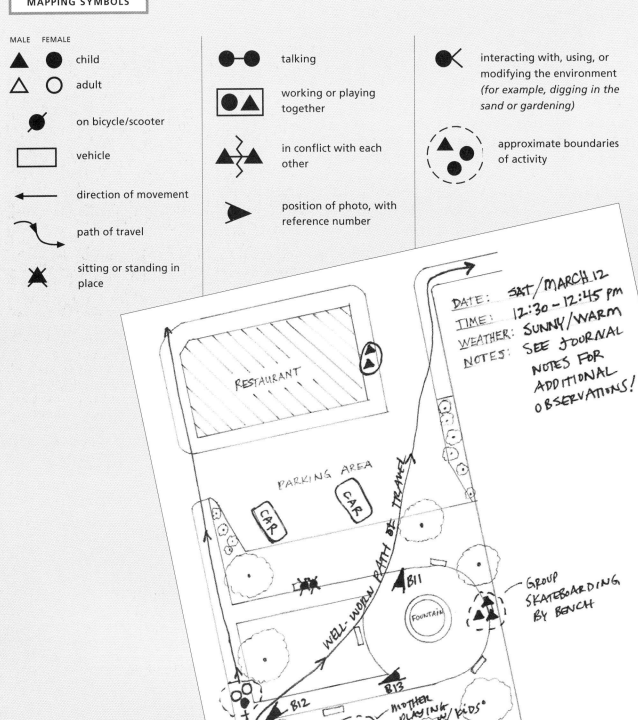

MAPPING SYMBOLS

MALE   FEMALE

▲   ● child

△   ○ adult

● on bicycle/scooter

▭ vehicle

← direction of movement

↝ path of travel

✖ sitting or standing in place

●—● talking

▣ working or playing together

▲⚡▲ in conflict with each other

◆ position of photo, with reference number

◆← interacting with, using, or modifying the environment *(for example, digging in the sand or gardening)*

⬚ approximate boundaries of activity

METHOD

Questionnaires and Surveys

Questionnaires and surveys are used to reach large numbers of people to obtain their input on key issues or ideas. Questionnaires can be useful early in the participation process to generate a complete list of issues of concern and a general understanding of the relative importance of issues among young people or the local population as a whole. Surveys require considerable work to ensure a representative sample and are therefore best used later in the process, once it is possible to frame meaningful questions or present specific project proposals for consideration and feedback. Questionnaires can also be valuable later in the process, but do not carry the same 'statistical validity' as surveys in providing feedback on specific issues, ideas or proposals. Questionnaires and surveys can be developed and implemented by project team members or by groups of young people who want to collect information from their peers or from other age groups.

Questionnaires and surveys can be conducted face-to-face or by telephone as a structured interview, or they can be distributed by mail or other means, filled out, and returned.

Questionnaires and surveys should not be the primary means of data collection and evaluation. They can enhance a participatory process, but are not in themselves conducive to the types of interaction and discussion that are necessary for a successful participation programme.

PURPOSE

> Involve a large number of people in giving input on project-related issues.
> Document community sentiment on key issues of concern.
> Provide statistically valid results to help to determine and support key project directions.

TIME REQUIRED

Questionnaires and surveys can be time-consuming, requiring anywhere from several weeks to several months to complete (depending on the number of people involved). Both questionnaires and surveys require time to develop the set of questions, conduct pre-testing, and to collect, tabulate and analyse results. Conducting a questionnaire or survey face-to-face requires a large team of people, training, coordination, and time spent

Questionnaires and Surveys

What is the difference between questionnaires, surveys and interviews?

The terms 'questionnaire' and 'survey' are often used interchangeably, and it is sometimes not clear how they might differ from an 'interview'. Indeed, they all share a common trait: they are systematic methods for gathering information, usually carried out using an established set of questions and through face-to-face interaction between an 'interviewer' (or 'surveyor') and a respondent.

While the terms are often used interchangeably, this manual uses specific definitions to differentiate between them.

- **Interview.** Interviews are a *systematic method* for gathering *qualitative information* from a relatively *small sample* of individuals. They can be formal, making use of a structured or semi-structured interview instrument, or relatively informal and unstructured (and less systematic) in an extended form of conversation. Interviews are typically conducted with a relatively small sample of key individuals or stakeholders. *Open-ended questions* and 'probing' questions are used to support *in-depth discussions* on key issues.

- **Questionnaire.** Like an interview, a questionnaire uses a *structured instrument* through which respondents answer a pre-set list of questions. However, it typically uses *close-ended questions* (such as multiple choice, yes/no, scale rating, or short answer) and does not

specifically support in-depth discussions or follow-up questions. Questionnaires are designed for use with *larger samples,* with the *ability to easily quantify responses* (for example, 34 percent of the respondents said 'x' while 66 percent said 'y'). Questionnaires are often completed by an interviewer, but can also be completed by people on their own (and therefore sent by mail or distributed through other channels), where *as many people as possible are encouraged to respond.* While attention is given to documenting the profile of respondents, little to no effort is given to making sure that the profile matches that of the larger population or to ensuring a 'random sample' of respondents.

- **Survey.** A survey is similar to a questionnaire in its use of a *structured instrument,* use of *close-ended questions,* ability to accommodate relatively *large samples,* and *ability to easily quantify responses.* The primary difference is in the sampling techniques; with surveys, an emphasis is placed on achieving a *randomly generated, representative sample.* This means that the sample of people surveyed is representative of the larger population of interest, and that therefore it is *'statistically valid'* and it is possible to make *generalizations based on its results.*

going door-to-door to fill in the form with each individual or household. A mail-out or pick-up/drop-off form can save staff time and resources, but requires a high level of literacy in the target population and at least two to three weeks between the time of distribution and the deadline for submitting completed forms.

MATERIALS NEEDED

> Questionnaire or survey form (see page 144)
> Distribution plan (see page 142)
> Clipboards and pencils if conducting face-to-face or by phone; postage and self-addressed stamped envelope (optional) if sending by mail

MAXIMIZING YOUNG PEOPLE'S PARTICIPATION

> *Give a complete explanation.* Explain the purpose of the questionnaire or survey and how the information will be used.

> *Let young people decide.* Let young people identify the issues to be addressed in the questionnaire or survey, specific questions to include, and the parameters of the distribution plan.

> *Involve young people in conducting the questionnaire or survey.* Have young people help in conducting the questionnaire or survey. With proper training, this can provide an excellent opportunity for young people to interact with their peers and with adults in the community.

PROCESS GUIDE

1. **Define the approach.** Consider the resources available and what the goals are for a questionnaire or survey. To provide an opportunity for more young people to give input or to confirm information being collected through other methods, a questionnaire may be appropriate. If it is important to have results that can be taken as representative of the community concerned, or of a larger group of young people, then a survey will be necessary. Consider also the way in which the questionnaire or survey will be distributed and completed: face-to-face, phone, mail, or pick-up/drop-off.

2. **Develop the questionnaire or survey form.** This is the form containing the questions that people will answer. See 'Developing a questionnaire or survey form' (page 144) for instructions and sample questions.

3. **Pre-test the questionnaire or survey form.** Test the draft questionnaire or survey form with several people who are representative of the target group to see if they understand the questions and if the questions lead to the type of information being sought. This will also give members of the project staff a chance to practice face-to-face interviews.

   On the pre-test form, ask for feedback. Based on their feedback, it will probably be necessary to modify, delete or add questions. Questions may need to be re-worded or reordered if they are confusing. It may also be

What is a 'representative sample'

A 'representative sample' is a relatively small number of people who reflect the general composition of the larger population (for example, by age, ethnic group and/or income). By selecting members of the community at random and ensuring an approximate match between the profile of the sample group and the profile of the larger community, it is possible to generalize from the survey results of the sample group to what might be expected if everyone in the larger community were asked the same set of questions. *Because survey design and sampling procedures are relatively complicated subjects, it is highly recommended that your project team include a person with survey and statistical expertise, such as a social science researcher from a local university.* See also page 57, 'Developing a Representative Sample'.

Questionnaires and Surveys

necessary to reduce the length of the questionnaire or survey so that it is not too time-consuming.

4. **Develop a distribution plan and conduct training.** Consider how the questionnaire or survey form will be distributed, filled in and collected. For surveys, determine the sampling technique to be used, establish the number of respondents needed, and develop a sampling plan if necessary.

   For face-to-face questionnaires and surveys: Determine how many team members will be needed to carry out face-to-face interviews. Train them on how to conduct the questionnaire or survey, and develop a plan for reaching people (typically door-to-door). Be sure to conduct the questionnaire or survey at different times of day and on different days of the week to provide a wide range of respondents.

   For telephone questionnaires and surveys: The same issues apply as for face-to-face interviews in terms of staff training and variation in the times of day. Logistics in terms of telephone operations must also be defined: How will you get the phone numbers of people in the local area? How will you manage the team making the phone calls?

   For mail-out questionnaires and surveys: Addresses and postage will be needed. Check for any specific mailing requirements and rates. Also, clearly print on the form where people are supposed to return it and the deadline for sending it in. To make it easier for respondents to send in their form, design the questionnaire with the return address printed on it so that it can be folded and posted, or provide a self-addressed stamped envelope.

   For pick-up/drop-off questionnaires and surveys: Determine how the survey or questionnaire forms will be made available (dropped off at every home? distributed at the local market? sent home with students through school?). Also, clearly print on the form where people are supposed to return it and the deadline for responses.

   Whichever technique is used, consider strategies for ensuring a high response rate. One such strategy is to send out a postcard in advance, notifying people that the questionnaire or survey will be coming soon and why it is important. Follow-up postcards can be sent later to remind respondents when the questionnaire or survey is due.

5. **Conduct the survey or questionnaire.** Print and distribute the questionnaire or survey. Encourage respondents to answer all the questions and to write clearly and legibly — especially for open-ended questions.

6. **Collect and tabulate results.** Number the questionnaire or survey forms as they come in, and organize them in files or binders. Establish a system for tabulating responses (ideally in an electronic spreadsheet program) and begin entering responses as soon as possible (see 'Tabulating results' on the facing page).

7. **Compile and display the results.** Once all the results are collected, they need to be compiled, analysed and summarized to identify major areas of consensus, areas of differing opinions, and any overall direction that may be emerging. Most spreadsheet programs have functions that will display numerical data in graphic formats that can be useful in the data analysis as well as in communicating the findings to others.

Tabulating Results

To tabulate the results of a questionnaire or survey, assign a reference number to each question and a unique code to each potential response. If you have access to a computer and software, set up a spreadsheet in which to enter the responses, using the columns for the survey question numbers and individual rows to code the responses from each survey form. Once all the responses are coded, you can run basic statistical analyses using the spreadsheet's built-in functions, such as counting the frequency of each response (the number of times a response was given), calculating the median (mid-point) or mean (average) responses, or conducting basic cross-tabulations (for example, analysing responses by gender, age or location). You can also quickly display the results in a 'bar graph' or 'pie chart' format.

If you do not have access to a computer, you can do the same type of coding and analysis manually, although doing cross-tabulations can be much more time-consuming. The most common calculation for each question will be the frequency of response. If the survey results were numerical (for example, asking people to rate something on a scale from 1 to 5), then it will be useful to calculate the average of the responses.

As survey tabulation and statistical analysis can be relatively complicated, it is advisable to consult with a person with relevant experience, drawing upon resources at a local college or university if possible.

© DAVID DRISKELL

Sathyanagar Resident Survey

The Growing Up in Cities site in Bangalore, India, conducted a door-to-door survey of community residents to establish baseline data as part of a comprehensive community planning effort. The survey covered basic demographic data (number and ages of people in the household, occupations, language, etc.) as well as planning issues and concerns about the community environment.

Questionnaires and Surveys

Developing a questionnaire or survey form

The success of a questionnaire or survey relies largely on the content, structure and style of its presentation. It must take respondents through a logical sequence of questions, maintain an objective and unbiased tone, allow for a complete range of potential responses, cover all the critical issues and perspectives, and (very important) remain concise and simple in its presentation so that people can fill it in on their own, completely and accurately.

To help to ensure an effective questionnaire or survey form, establish a working group of project team members and local young people to formulate the questions and format and conduct the pre-testing.

QUESTION TOPICS

Clarify the purpose of the survey and develop a list of the general topic areas that the form will cover. Try to keep the list of general topic areas brief, remembering that the shorter the form the more likely people will be to fill it in.

The potential effectiveness of a questionnaire or survey will increase later in the project when there is a stronger sense of key issues and alternatives on which you wish to have feedback. If you do not have a clear idea of the question topics, review the list of potential interview topics on pages 110–111.

The following sections should be included in almost all questionnaires or surveys:

- **Explanation and instructions.** Be sure to include an opening section to introduce respondents to the questionnaire or survey purpose, provide instructions for filling it in, assure respondents of anonymity, and identify a place or person to contact if they have questions.

- **Respondent profile.** Include a section for collecting basic background information on respondents, such as age, gender and area in which they live (nearest street intersection, for example) so that you can compare the profile of people who responded with the overall profile of people in the community. This is particularly important for surveys, where a representative sample is required. Do not ask for people's names, addresses or telephone numbers. It is likely to discourage them from being completely open and honest in their responses, and may deter them from participating altogether.

- **Thanks.** Include a brief statement at the end thanking people for their participation and, if applicable, telling them where to return completed forms and the deadline for responses. If the survey or questionnaire is to be mailed in, design it so that it can be folded and posted, with the address pre-printed on it.

Questionnaires and Surveys

QUESTION FORMATS

Questionnaires and surveys typically use close-ended questions to make it possible for a large number of responses to be easily tabulated and quantified. The format for the questions may vary considerably, as shown in the following examples. In determining which format or combination of formats to use, consider the way in which the form will be filled in (individually, face-to-face, by phone) and the level of familiarity that people in the local area might have with this method. In all cases, keep the form as simple and as short as possible, and pre-test it to remove any confusion in the content, style or format of the questions.

Question formats to consider include:

- **Multiple choice.** This format presents a question or statement followed by several possible responses, from which the respondent is typically expected to select one response (although it can also be structured to allow them to select more than one response). For example:

Our neighbourhood is undergoing many changes. If you could travel ten years into the future and see the changes that have taken place, do you think our neighbourhood will be (circle one answer):

A) better than it is today   C) about the same as it is today

B) worse than it is today   D) no opinion

All multiple-choice questions should provide respondents with a way to voice their disagreement with or lack of opinion about the potential responses, such as 'None of the above' or 'No opinion'.

- **Ranking.** This format provides a list of potential responses and asks the respondent to rank them in order or to select a limited number from the larger list. For example:

What do you think are the three most important issues that need to be addressed in your local area? Please write a '1' next to what you think is most important, a '2' next to the second most important, and a '3' next to the third most important.

___ clean the streets   ___ attract new businesses

___ provide better schools   ___ improve the water quality

___ rebuild the health centre   ___ other _____

___ create a small garden or park   ___ other _____

___ train people for better jobs

Ranking exercises can be made more approachable in face-to-face interviews by having a set of cards with the responses written or illustrated on them. The respondent is then asked to sort the cards with the most important on the top and the least important on the bottom. Regardless of the specific technique, be sure to include 'other' as a

Questionnaires and Surveys

response option so that respondents can add their own response if it does not match the pre-selected list.

- **Agree/Disagree.** This is perhaps the most common form of question, in which respondents are read a question or statement to which they may respond 'yes/agree' or 'no/disagree'. For example:

Are the streets in our area safe at night? (yes or no?)

Alternatively, a more complex but perhaps more revealing method is to provide a scale for indicating agreement or disagreement. For example:

Please read the following series of statements. For each one, please indicate whether you:
1) STRONGLY AGREE **2)** SOMEWHAT AGREE **3)** HAVE NO OPINION **4)** SOMEWHAT DISAGREE **5)** STRONGLY DISAGREE

The streets in our area are safe at night.   1   2   3   4   5

This can be a useful format when a series of alternative proposals are being considered. After reading each strategy, respondents can indicate their level of support (or opposition) rather than simply saying they like it or do not like it. An alternative scale in this case might be from '1' for 'I think it is a very good proposal' to '5' for 'I am opposed to this proposal'.

To make it easier for people to rank each statement during a face-to-face interview, provide a set of cards with the numbers and rankings written on them to use to 'vote' on each statement. The cards can be simplified with symbols indicating support (such as a smiling face) or opposition (a frown), with a small smile, no expression and small frown used for other levels on the scale.

- **Short answer.** In this format, respondents are asked to give very brief responses to a question. For example:

What are your three favourite things about our neighbourhood?
1. _____
2. _____
3. _____

- **Open-ended/long answer.** These types of question may be useful or necessary to allow people to give longer, more in-depth feedback on key areas of concern. However, in general try to avoid the use of open-ended questions as each written response must be reviewed and coded to identify key ideas and themes, making tabulation and analysis time-consuming. At most, include one or two such questions in a survey or questionnaire. The interview questions listed on pages 110–111 are all examples of open-ended questions.

Questionnaires and Surveys

METHOD

Focus Groups and Small-Group Discussions[4]

Focus groups and other forms of small-group discussions are useful early in the participation process to identify key issues and to understand group dynamics. They are also useful later in the process to discuss the results of previous data-collection efforts and to develop a group consensus on a course of action. How-
ever, group discussion formats also have drawbacks in that some members of the group may dominate the discussion, and there may be a tendency to gloss over differences, avoiding in-depth exploration of issues in favour of group harmony. With this in mind, it is best to include both group and individual methods in any participatory process. Other group methods in this manual include 'Role-play, drama and puppetry' (page 124) and 'Workshops and community events' (page 154). There are also methods that lend themselves to either an individual or group approach, including 'Guided tours' (page 127), 'Drawings' (page 115) and 'Photographs by young people' (page 130).

After a series of walking tours in the local area, workshop participants in Waginengen, the Netherlands, have a small group discussion about the places they visited and why, providing an initial compilation and comparison of their individual evaluations of the local area.

PURPOSE

> Engage a small group (six to ten individuals) in a discussion on local issues.
> Understand community knowledge, ideas, attitudes and feelings.
> Develop constructive group dialogue and build consensus.
> Collectively explore and analyse the results of previous participation activities.
> Agree upon a course of action in response to identified issues.

TIME REQUIRED

The time required for a small-group discussion will vary depending on the number of people involved, their familiarity with each other, and the meeting agenda. Time for meeting preparation and follow-up is essential. A successful two-hour meeting typically requires that much or more preparation time beforehand and follow-up afterwards. Also, if the group has never met before, time for introductions and 'ice-breaking' will be needed during the meeting itself.

MATERIALS NEEDED

> Quiet place to meet that is large enough to comfortably accommodate all the participants
> Method for recording the group discussion (wall graphic, flip chart, notebook, or tape recorder). See 'Creating a group memory', page 152.
> Additional equipment as necessary to support the meeting's activities

MAXIMIZING YOUNG PEOPLE'S PARTICIPATION

> *Give a complete explanation.* Explain the purpose of the small-group session and how the information that is collected will be used.
> *Allow enough time.* Provide adequate time for the group to explore the issues of concern to them.
> *Let young people lead.* Allow young people to determine the meeting agenda and the topics to be discussed. Work with them to develop skills in facilitation and recording and allow them to run the group discussion sessions on their own.
> *Do not dictate or judge outcomes.* Focus on listening to young people's perceptions and their ideas regarding potential responses to identified issues. Give input only when requested, and try to be as objective as possible so that your own biases do not direct the group discussion in one way or another.

What is a 'focus group'?

A focus group is a particular kind of small-group discussion involving a *select group* of individuals in a *facilitated discussion* about a topic or set of topics established either by the facilitator or by the group members themselves. Participants are selected because they share *similar characteristics* (such as working children or teenagers or single mothers), providing an opportunity to understand their *knowledge, attitudes and feelings* about the topic(s) at hand. Participants are encouraged to express their views and feelings about the issue or topic in their own words, exploring the issue in some depth and, at times, responding to the input given by other participants. A focus group is a *data-collection tool,* not a consensus-building tool. However, it is not a group interview. It is a directed dialogue in which the interaction between participants may be as revealing as what is actually said by each individual. Focus groups *typically meet once only,* though it is possible that they could meet consecutively over a period of time to explore an issue or sequence of issues in depth.

PROCESS GUIDE

1. **Define the format, group size, agenda and staffing needs.** Small-group discussions can take a variety of forms. Basic criteria to consider are:

   > *How will the participants be selected?* Some groups should be carefully selected to represent a particular part of the population (as in a focus group, see previous page) while others can be open to whoever wishes to participate.

   > *How many participants?* A small group is, by definition, limited to a small number of participants, typically between six and ten. If there are many more than ten participants, the quality of the group discussion may deteriorate, with some participants not having an opportunity to speak and/or the discussion taking so long that everyone loses interest. To open the process to everyone who wishes to participate, convene first one large group and then divide into small groups, with a facilitator and recorder for each. Small groups can then reconvene to share the results of their discussions with each other.

   > *How will the discussion be organized?* Will there be a set agenda for the discussion, with predetermined topics, or will it be more free-flowing? Who should be involved in helping to set the agenda? Are there opportunities for participants to be involved in the agenda-setting process?

   > *How often will the group meet?* Will the group meet only once, or will there be ongoing meetings to work through various issues and build consensus? The advantage of ongoing meetings is that the group is able to explore issues in greater depth and to develop relationships within the group that may facilitate more open and honest communication as well as a stronger commitment to the task and to each other.

   > *How many facilitators and recorders will you need?* Each small-group session should be facilitated and recorded. These roles may be played by project staff or by local young people, keeping in mind that neither the facilitator nor the recorder should be an active participant in the discussion and all facilitators and recorders should be properly trained for their roles. See 'Being an effective facilitator' on page 151 and 'Creating a group memory' on page 152.

2. **Train staff as necessary.** It is important that each small group be facilitated and recorded. Staff facilitators and recorders need to be trained in their roles and must understand the purpose and structure of the meeting as well as, ideally, the composition and dynamics of the group involved. In general, it is helpful if the participants are familiar and comfortable with the facilitator. However, in some situations there may be value in having a facilitator who is not known to the group to provide a 'neutral' setting in which participants may freely speak their minds.

3. **Select the location and schedule the meeting.** Hold the session in a quiet location that is conveniently accessible to participants, free from interruptions and large

Focus Groups and Small-Group Discussions

Informal and spontaneous small-group discussions

Young people engage in an informal discussion regarding their plans for a community exhibit.

This 'Process guide' focuses on relatively structured forms of small-group discussions. However, small-group sessions can also be spontaneous and informal, especially with groups of young people who know each other well or have been working together for a time. Skilled facilitators can quickly organize sessions to discuss issues as they arise in the course of other participatory activities, facilitating relatively brief discussions of 20 to 30 minutes so that group members can share their thoughts and perspectives with each other 'in the moment' rather than waiting a week to discuss them in a separate session. Over time, meeting and sharing in small-group discussions will become a natural part of the group's dynamics, and young people may begin to organize themselves in spontaneous sessions, taking turns as facilitators and recorders.

enough to hold everyone comfortably in a large circle or semi-circle. Schedule the session at a time that will not conflict with participants' other commitments.

4. **Establish ground rules.** Ask participants to agree upon a basic set of ground rules for the meeting at the beginning of the session. Either allow participants to define their own rules, or develop a list of basic rules beforehand and ask them to review, modify and confirm them.

5. **Facilitate and record the session.** Begin the small-group session by defining and agreeing upon the purpose and focus of the session and the length of the meeting. If there is to be an agenda, agree on what it will be and write it on a large board or sheet of paper so that everyone can follow it. Introduce the facilitator and recorder, explaining the role of each, and ask each participant to introduce him or herself. In groups where participants are not familiar with each other, consider having a fun activity at the beginning that might help people to learn more about each other.

6. **Summarize the results and follow up with participants.** End meetings on time, with clear agreement on what will happen next. Thank participants for their time and input, and be sure that they understand how the meeting's results will be summarized and used. If the results are to be shared with others, ask for their permission and be sure to follow whatever confidentiality agreement has been reached with the group (see page 92). Be sure to record the date and time and place of the meeting, and the names of the participants (if appropriate). If a written summary of meeting results is prepared, make it available to the group participants.

Being an effective facilitator

The facilitator is responsible for making sure that the group discussion goes smoothly, remains focused on the agreed topic(s), and finishes on time. The facilitator helps to make sure that everyone has a chance to speak and that no one person or group of people dominates the discussion. The facilitator also helps to set the tone for the group discussion and provides the 'glue' that keeps the group together. If the facilitator has low energy and seems disinterested, the chances are that the rest of the group will too. The facilitator may also have to play the role of mediator, helping to resolve conflicts if they arise.

Facilitators do not bring their own perspective into the discussions. However, they may play a role in identifying common themes, linkages or contradictions between points being raised. They may also have to direct discussions to make sure that all relevant points are addressed.

The level and style of facilitation that is necessary will vary by group and culture, with factors such as age and gender playing a role in establishing group dynamics. Groups that have developed a good working rapport will require little facilitation, while contentious groups will require active facilitation. Likewise, in some cultures participating in a free exchange of ideas in a group setting may be a common practice, while in others it may make people uncomfortable.

Some key points that facilitators should keep in mind include:
> Always explain your role as the facilitator.
> Make sure that everyone is familiar with the ground rules for the group discussion and the purpose of the session.
> Emphasize that there are no 'right' or 'wrong' answers. The purpose of the session is to share and discuss each other's ideas and opinions.
> Never dominate the group discussion, offer your own opinions, correct what people in the group have said, or act as the 'expert'.
> Encourage everyone to listen and keep an open mind.
> Listen.
> Make sure all participants are involved and that all contributions are valued.
> Maintain a high energy level and positive attitude.
> Be sensitive to cultural traditions and norms for group interaction.
> Make participants feel comfortable and at ease.
> Organize the group so that everyone has eye contact with each other (in a circle or semi-circle).
> Summarize key points, highlighting common themes and linkages between ideas as well as differences of opinion.
> Intervene to head off inappropriate behaviour that violates the group's ground rules, including domination of the discussion by one or more individuals.

Focus Groups and Small-Group Discussions

Creating a group memory

The traditional method of recording group comments is to take written notes. However, it is sometimes difficult to capture everything that is said, and the fact that only the note-taker can see the notes means that no one else in the group can correct incomplete or inaccurate notes during the course of the meeting.

Newer methods of recording include tape recording and/or videotape recording. These help to ensure that participants' inputs are captured vividly and accurately. However, they require considerable time to transcribe the tape or video into a written transcript of the discussion. Both tape and video recording can also be disruptive to the group process, especially with young people who may be distracted by the novelty of being recorded.

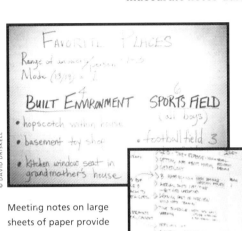

Meeting notes on large sheets of paper provide a 'group memory' that helps to keep the group's discussion focused and ensure that key points are accurately recorded.

Another method of recording relies on taking 'group notes' or creating what might be called a 'group memory' of the discussion. This is most commonly done on large sheets of paper on an easel. However, a more effective method of taking group notes is to create a 'wall graphic' on large sheets of newsprint or other inexpensive paper (ideally 1 m high by 3 to 4 m long) taped to a wall at the front of the group before the meeting starts. This provides a large note-taking surface where the entire discussion can be recorded, allowing everyone to see the summary of the group's discussion in a single place. (Be sure to put at least two layers of paper so that the marker ink does not go through on to the wall surface.) In some places, large sheets of newsprint can be obtained from local printers who may be willing to donate remnant newsprint rolls or sell them at a discount.

A skilled 'graphic recorder' can capture the group's comments in both text and sketches on a large wall graphic, using different-coloured marking pens to highlight key points, illustrate connections, and define areas of disagreement. The use of graphics and simple drawings can help to illustrate the discussion's results.

Field trips and photos to see new possibilities

Several Growing Up in Cities sites took small groups of young people from the local area on field trips to nearby areas to see examples of other places near where they live.

- **In Oakland,** where young people expressed a desire to improve the courtyard of their housing development as a play area, photographs and slides were shown of playgrounds and public spaces around the world so that they could see that the ground is not always covered with concrete, trees are not always fenced, gardens can have flowers, and benches or other outdoor furniture can invite people to socialize. The children then went to visit some of the play areas, community gardens and murals in Oakland and San Francisco that they had first seen in the slides. They later developed models to explore different design ideas for their own courtyard space.

- **In Göteburg,** after young people in three different neighbourhoods had evaluated their local environment using participatory methods, a series of neighbourhood exchanges were conducted so that they could share information about their local areas and ideas for change. The young people then prepared a combined exhibit at the Municipal Museum, entitled 'Under Ytan' (Under the Surface). During an afternoon programme of events, about a hundred people gathered to see and hear what they had done and their ideas for local improvements. In conclusion, chairpersons from the three districts discussed how the project would be carried forward.

Participants in the Streetspace project spent a day visiting active street spaces and playgrounds around the local area.

- **In Melbourne,** participants in the 'Streetspace' project (see page 171) spent a day visiting active street spaces and playgrounds around the local area so that they could experience spaces which work for people, and places that are popular with young people, including an adventure playground that was 'over the bridge' from their own neighbourhood. The places they saw on their field trip then informed the participatory design process they were engaged in (using a large three-dimensional model of their neighbourhood) for improvements in their own area.

© KAREN MALONE

Focus Groups and Small-Group Discussions

METHOD

Workshops and Community Events

This covers a broad range of group activities that are geared towards community interaction, information sharing, discussion and decision-making. They are typically highly visible events that help to develop community awareness and promote consensus building.

© DAVID DRISKELL

Such events are extremely useful later in the process as a means of communicating young people's perspectives to the community, promoting a broader discussion of possible strategies, and developing a community consensus for action. They can also be useful early in the process for gathering input from the larger community and fostering public awareness of the project and key issues. Regardless of when they take place, community events should always be structured and implemented in ways that achieve real participation for young people (see 'Making young people's participation real', page 40).

A community event at the Growing Up in Cities site in Bangalore, India, provided an opportunity to share young people's work, acknowledge their input, and discuss ways of moving forward.

PURPOSE

> Gather input from a large cross-section of the community.

> Engage a large group in a discussion on local issues.

> Understand community knowledge, ideas, attitudes and feelings.

> Communicate young people's views and the information they have developed to the community at large and key decision-makers.

> Collectively explore and analyse the results of previous participation activities.

> Broaden the dialogue on key issues and potential courses of action to the larger community.

> Agree upon a course of action in response to identified issues.

> Build community-wide consensus for action.

TIME REQUIRED

The time required for a workshop or special event varies considerably depending on the scope and scale of the event. As in all participation activities, preparation is critical and requires more time than most people usually anticipate. A workshop of several hours may require a week or more of preparation time, as well as time after the event to summarize and distribute the results and take other follow-up actions.

MATERIALS NEEDED

The materials for a large group will vary according to the particular activities being under-taken. However, some basic items should always be considered (though they may not always be needed, available or appropriate):

> Name tags if people do not know each other
> Sign-in sheet (to have a record of who was there and to send follow-up materials and future announcements)
> A method for recording group discussions (wall graphic, flip chart, notebook or tape recorder). See 'Creating a group memory', page 152.
> Refreshments (drinks, snacks)
> Accessible restrooms

MAXIMIZING YOUNG PEOPLE'S PARTICIPATION

> *Give a complete explanation.* Explain the purpose and expected outcomes of the work-shop or community event and the roles that different people will play in making it happen.

> *Let young people lead.* Allow young people to take the lead in planning for and imple-menting the workshop or community event. At a minimum, involve them as active par-ticipants in the planning process along with adult members of the project team and then encourage them to play an active role in the workshop or event itself, interacting with other members of the larger community.

> *Give young people a voice.* If part of the workshop or community event involves a pre-sentation regarding young people's perspectives and ideas, encourage them to organize and present the information themselves, providing assistance as they request it (or if they refuse help, get out of the way and let them do their work). Strive to communicate information to the larger community using young people's own words, photographs, pictures and related materials.

PROCESS GUIDE

Workshops and special events vary widely in format, scale and structure. Some examples are provided beginning on page 157. The following are some general procedural notes to consider.

1. Define the format, agenda and staffing needs

> *What is the purpose of the activity?* Clearly define what the activity aims to achieve. Is it to raise community awareness? A data-collection activity? A chance to explore options and strategies? A consensus-building activity?

> *How many people do you expect?* Consider all the stakeholder groups who may be in-terested in participating, as well as people who may not be interested but should be

Workshops and Community Events

encouraged to participate. Determine the maximum number of people you can realistically expect to participate and plan accordingly.

> *How will people be notified?* Schedule the event at a time when the people who you hope will attend will be available. Plan well in advance of the actual date so that adequate notice can be given to potential participants.

> *Where will the event take place?* The activity should be held in an accessible and convenient location within the community. Do not expect people to travel a long distance to participate, but also make sure that the activity can be accommodated in the place it is being held. It may be necessary to modify the event to fit the place if it is important to meet in a specific location.

> *What will be the agenda of activities?* How long will the event be, and what sorts of activities are planned to achieve the stated goals? Who should be involved in setting the agenda? Are there opportunities for young participants to be involved in the planning process?

> *How many staff will you need?* Consider the activities that are planned and the number of staff required, including facilitators and recorders for both large-group and small-group discussions.

2. **Train staff as necessary.** Make sure that everyone who will be involved understands the purpose of the event and their role in it. Provide training as needed for staff.

3. **Publicize the event.** Get word out early and often about the activity, including information on why it is being held and the details on where and when. Utilize existing community information channels such as noticeboards, local newspapers, and the bulletins of local organizations.

4. **Be prepared well in advance.** Make sure you have all the necessary materials and that the location is set up well in advance of the actual beginning of the event. Have everyone who is helping meet beforehand to review their roles, the agenda of activities, and the room or site set-up.

An 'accordion' meeting format begins with a large group, breaks into smaller groups and then reconvenes as a large group to share results.

5. **Facilitate and record the workshop or event.** If the community event includes group discussions, ensure that they are properly facilitated and recorded. Always consider breaking large groups into several smaller groups so that everyone can have a chance to participate, unless there is an advantage in remaining as a large group.

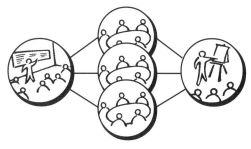

LARGE-GROUP
INTRODUCTION

SMALL-GROUP
DISCUSSIONS

LARGE-GROUP
SHARING

Workshops and
Community Events

6. **Focus on participation.** Encourage the participation of everyone present. Do not let the event become a forum for presentations, lectures and other forms of 'teaching'. The emphasis should be on learning from each other, giving everyone an opportunity to be an active participant. While some presentation time may be necessary, it should not be the focus of the event.

7. **Summarize the results and follow up with participants.** End the event on time, and close with clear agreement on what will happen next. Thank participants for their time and input, and be sure that they understand how the results will be summarized and used. If the results are to be shared with others, ask for their permission and be sure to follow whatever confidentiality agreement exists (see page 92). If a written summary is being prepared, make it available to the participants.

The city as a living museum[5]

In this activity, members of the community (young people or a mix of ages) explore the local area and select interesting, intriguing or unusual spots. They then place large 'frames' (which can be made of stiff cardboard and painted white or a bright colour) at each spot, calling attention to a particular feature in the environment. The frames can be left there for a period of time, serving as the basis for a community 'gallery' or 'museum' tour. Alternatively, the frames can be held in place and a photograph can be taken of the frame and its contents. Stories about each spot are collected to serve as captions. In the case of a community museum tour, each spot is numbered and a 'museum cata-logue' is produced with a map showing the frame locations and a summary of their captions. In the case of the photography exhibit, the pictures are processed and displayed on large boards with their captions, serving as the basis for continued discussion about the area and the spots that were selected.

A frame is used to highlight an important feature in the local environment.

This is a fun activity that can foster a high level of community interaction and dialogue about the local area, both in the process of creating the exhibit (being in the streets) and in the review of the exhibit itself.

Workshops and Community Events

Young people in Buenos Aires, Argentina, prepare a large base map in a public plaza and then invite everyone to join in writing their memories and opinions on it.

© NILDA COSCO AND ROBIN MOORE

Gulliver's mapping[6]

This is a simple and fun activity that encourages residents of all ages to explore their memories, experiences and opinions about the local area. It can also be a highly visible activity that raises awareness and encourages dialogue about issues in the local environment.

© KAREN MALONE

Results from a Gulliver's Mapping exercise in Melbourne, Australia.

A large map (1:250 to 1:500 scale) of the local area is displayed and residents are invited to make any kind of comment they want on it. The activity takes place over the course of about ten days in a visible public location (such as a shopping centre or community centre). Ideally, the map is installed on the floor and people are invited to take off their shoes and walk or kneel on it to write their comments. There should also be wall space all around where additional information can be displayed or comments recorded, and enough room to accommodate dozens of people.

As comments begin to fill the map, close-up photographs are taken of the map space. These photographs focus attention on specific sites in the local area and their special meanings. These are Gulliver's Footprints — the individual and collective memories and meanings associated with places in the local urban habitat. The photographs, or Gulliver Cards, help to document the mapping results, and can serve as the basis for a photo gallery on the local environment as well as for site visits that can provide an opportunity to photograph the actual sites and to share more stories about each place. An exhibit in conjunction with the map can be developed over the course of the week, with footprint exhibits and map locations cross-referenced. The exhibit can then be placed in a public place — such as a city hall or community centre — to foster further discussion.

Through the process of Gulliver's Mapping, residents collectively put down their memories, experiences and opinions about the place where they live, developing a deeper understanding of their environment and each other. As Junzo Okada, one of the method's originators, quotes from the Japanese film-maker Akira Kurosawa — 'Memory is the basis for everything'.

Workshops and Community Events

Community design workshop

A participatory community design workshop can help to define an appropriate design response to issues identified in the local environment. Such workshops involve users of the environment in an interactive process to define project goals, explore possible design alternatives, and define a preferred design that best meets the community's needs. Depending on the scale and scope of the project, these tasks may be achieved in a single all-day workshop, or over the course of several meetings. Regardless of the scale and scope of the project, young people should be involved as integral participants in the design and decision-making process.

Such workshops typically involve planning or design professionals as resources for the community process. They provide information on available design technologies and examples of projects undertaken by other communities. They can also serve as a sounding board for the community's ideas. However, it is important that professional resource people respect the community process and their role in it. They are there to supply technical information to support informed decision-making, not as experts on what is best for the community.

A design workshop may take many forms, from small projects in an individual building to large projects that affect and involve the entire community. In every case, the participation of all affected user groups is critical to a successful design outcome. Also, regardless of the scale and format of the workshop, the basic process will involve:

- **Review of the existing area.** This may involve participants in evaluation activities similar to those described earlier in this chapter (such as interviews, guided tours, and

© ROBIN MOORE

Young people in the Boca-Barracas area of Buenos Aires, Argentina, identified *baldíos* (vacant lots) in their neighbourhood that provided opportunities for improvement. They then conducted field investigations of each site, interviewed local residents about their ideas, developed design programmes, and prepared schematic design sketches and three-dimensional models to illustrate their proposals to their friends, parents, and community residents. Their proposals were also displayed at the Buenos Aires Cultural Centre.

Workshops and Community Events

behaviour mapping) to develop a clear understanding of what is working about the area currently, and opportunities for improvement.

• **Agreement on the 'design programme'.** A design programme describes the physical and programmatic goals for improvement of an area — what types of use or activity should be accommodated, and what facilities are desired? How many people are to be served? Are there special needs that must be considered, based on age or ability? Will the use of the space vary by day of the week or time of day? How will potentially conflicting uses (such as sports activities versus social activities) be reconciled? The exploration of design alternatives may help to resolve some of the design programme issues, but a basic understanding of the design goals is needed before alternatives can be defined.

• **Exploration of alternative design strategies.** The process should encourage creative thinking and problem solving in the exploration of design alternatives. Different groups may wish to develop different design approaches to provide a range of options for further review and discussion, with evaluation of the strengths and weaknesses of each option.

• **Definition of a preferred design strategy.** Using the evaluation results from the exploration of alternatives, a preferred design strategy can be developed that best meets the requirements of all user groups as defined in the design programme.

Several of the Growing Up in Cities sites engaged young people in participatory workshops to develop proposals for public spaces identified by young people as being important to them and in need of improvement, such as the 'Streetspace' project in Melbourne, Australia (see page 171), and the development of design proposals for vacant lots in the Boca-Barracas area of Buenos Aires, Argentina (see photo above).

ENDNOTES

1 From *I Was a Savage,* as quoted in Edmund Carpenter, *Oh, What a Blow that Phantom Gave Me*, p. 78, New York, Holt, Rinehart and Winston, 1972.

2 See *Growing Up in Cities* (Kevin Lynch, editor; 1977) in Appendix B, Resources.

3 Adapted from material provided by Jill Swart-Kruger, South Africa Director for Growing Up in Cities.

4 Adapted from material provided by Barry Percy-Smith of Nene College, Northampton, UK, leader of the UK GUIC site.

5 Landscape architect Dr Isami Kinoshita of the Taishido Study Group in Setagaya Ward, Tokyo, originally developed this activity under the title 'Street Art Workshop'. It has been adapted based on material provided by Robin Moore and Nilda Cosco of the Argentine GUIC site.

6 Masahiro Nakamura of the Taishido Study Group in Setagaya Ward, Tokyo, originally developed this activity for an exhibit entitled 'Experiences of Urbanism by Mapping'. It was further developed by Junzo Okada and has been adapted based on material provided by Robin Moore and Nilda Cosco of the Argentine GUIC site.

Making Change Happen

Children in Johannesburg, South Africa, discuss their ideas for improving their local area.

© MELINDA SWIFT

CHAPTER SEVEN

Never doubt that a small group of thoughtful committed citizens can change the world: indeed, it's the only thing that ever has.

MARGARET MEAD

As emphasized throughout this manual, the ultimate goal of participatory community development projects is to make change happen. In addition to discussing their experiences and ideas about the local area, young people should be involved in deciding what to do with the information that has been collected, and in developing and carrying out a plan for change. This final chapter discusses how to translate the results of a participatory evaluation into an action programme, and how to realize the benefits of the participatory learning process for future projects and activities.

Analysing the Results

Through participatory evaluation, your team will collect and create various types of information, from drawings and photographs to interview results and project team diary notes. To be of use, this information must be carefully analysed to identify themes and patterns in the data that will help to define key issues that need to be addressed.

The following suggestions will help to ensure an effective analysis process.

- **Involve an experienced researcher.** The assistance of experienced social science researchers or other skilled persons can be extremely helpful in organizing and analysing the project data. Ideally, these individuals would have been involved throughout the process. They can help to make sure that interview instruments are as unbiased as possible, that the collected data are being properly organized and archived, and that the data analysis is thorough and objective. They may also have statistical skills or experience in analytical methods.

- **Make it participatory.** Although the process of 'data analysis' may sound technical and potentially daunting, it is something in which everyone can and should be involved. Experienced researchers can be very valuable in helping to organize and direct the analysis effort, but they should not conduct the analysis on their own. The involvement of other project team members and local young people in the process can help to ensure that the data are not misunderstood and that interpretation is not skewed by the bias of one person or an adult-centred perspective.

- **Start early.** It is not necessary to wait until all the information is collected before beginning the data analysis. In fact, it can be helpful to conduct preliminary analyses early in the data-collection process. This may provide insights into ongoing project activities, and allow subsequent activities to be more closely tailored to the issues that are being identified. However, do not draw final conclusions from the first round of input alone and focus subsequent activities solely on those findings, especially when working with young people. As they become more comfortable with the project team and with expressing their feelings and ideas, new issues may come to light that differ from the first impressions. Allow the early analysis of data to inform the process, but not to control it.

• **Keep project information organized.** It is important to keep project data well organized and archived. Set up a workable system of organization at the very start of the project, and make sure that the project results are documented, labelled and filed at the end of each day. It takes much less time to organize files on a daily basis than to make sense of a jumbled pile of papers, photographs and other materials at the end of the project. See page 94 for tips on 'Keeping things organized'.

• **Make working copies, save the originals.** In the analysis process, it can be useful to mark on or even cut up pieces of information from the interviews, diaries, drawings and other data sources, making it easier to sort them in different ways or to explore possible

---

FIGURE 7

Examples of data tables

Perceived Changes in Powisle
Frequency of response among those who observed change (N=32; AGES=13–15)

CHANGES NOTICED BY CHILDREN	% OF CHILDREN
Changed street appearance	70
Changes in the natural environment	63
Renovated buildings	52
New buildings	41
New stores	41
New technical infrastructure (e.g.traffic lights)	38
General improvement in the look of the district	26
Demographic changes (more crowded streets, more strangers and poor people)	25
New recreational facilities for children and youth	25

What is the furthest place that you have been in Oakland?
(N = 28, 13males / 15 females)

Don't Know

Lake Tahoe, Nevada
San Leandro, California
Oakland Zoo
Church
Jack London Square

Pittsburg, California, Nevada, Lucky Store, San Francisco, Boston, Canada, Washington, Reno, 98th Avenue, Bay Bridge, Toys R Us, Cambodian store, Alameda, a store we drive to

Type size represents **11%**, 7%, 4%

Simply summarizing the results in table format can bring key findings to light and help people to see relationships between different data. Be sure to properly label the table, including its rows, columns and unit(s) of measurement as well as the sources of data and sample size, when relevant. The table above is from the GUIC site in Poland.

A summary of interview responses should indicate how many times each response was given. In the summary above from the GUIC site in the USA, the frequency of each response is represented by its relative type size. The more common the response, the larger its type size.

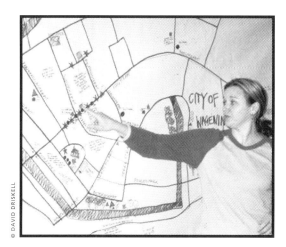

© DAVID DRISKELL

Project team members who had gone on walking tours in Waginengen, the Netherlands, compiled their individual tour results on a large map of the area, identifying the specific places they visited and young people's evaluation of those places. In less than an hour, common themes as well as differences are identified and documented through the project team's discussion.

themes and patterns. If possible, make a copy of the original data (interview instruments, note sheets, drawings, etc.) before marking or cutting up anything. Save the originals and work only on the copies. Before taking sheets apart, be sure that each page is marked with the title and date of the project activity, and any other pertinent information, so you can always be sure of where the information came from.

- **Identify key themes and patterns.** Explore the assembled data to identify recurring themes and key issues. Look for patterns by comparing the responses according to different variables such as age, gender, income, ethnicity, religion, location. Do boys tend to view issues differently to girls? Do older people tend to use a particular area differently to young people? This type of analysis can be time-consuming, but is indispensable in understanding the data and drawing meaningful conclusions. This is where the skills of an experienced researcher can be valuable.

- **Search for inter-relationships and causal factors.** Explore potential relationships between the different key issues as well as between different types of data. Is there anything in the data that might point to potential causes or provide a fuller understanding of the issue? For example, is there a connection between young people's use of a certain area and that area's physical characteristics? Is there a correlation between young people's attitudes about the future and their access to education, employment or other opportunities? The participation of people with different perspectives and professional backgrounds in the analysis process can be extremely useful in helping to explore these types of relationship. However, be careful not to assume a relationship where one may not actually exist. If the relationship seems to be important but the data is insufficient to draw a firm conclusion, consider conducting a follow-up activity to explore it further.

- **Look for hidden issues.** In addition to analysing what participants said, pay attention to what they did not say. Is there a mismatch between what project team members observed in the local area, and the descriptions or input of the participants? Was there a level of discomfort among participants in discussing certain issues? Were there inconsistencies between what participants said in the interview, and what was reflected in their guided tour, drawing, or other activities? Did people say one thing when talking one-to-one, and something else when talking in a group? These types of behaviour can be indicative of 'hidden' issues that participants did not discuss, for any number of reasons, but which may be extremely important in terms of understanding the local situation. However, extreme caution should be used when inferring the existence of a 'hidden issue'. It can be very easy to project one's own ideas and perspectives, inferring information, values and perspectives that might be quite different from what actually exist.

- **Keep an open mind.** A common pitfall in data analysis is to look only for the information that you already suspect you will find. This is usually done unintentionally, but in this process, the data is selectively analysed to justify foregone conclusions. Team members who have formed their opinions about what the key issues are over the course of the project will tend to see the same issues as they analyse the data. One solution is to involve a range of people and perspectives in the analysis process — including some people who have not been involved in the project thus far. Also, everyone involved in the data analysis should make a conscious effort to keep an open mind, searching for and being receptive to unexpected or even contradictory results.

- **Summarize and distribute the results.** The results of the analysis should be summarized and made available to the participants, the community at large, and relevant stakeholders and decision-makers. The summary should focus on the key findings and present them in an easy-to-read format, using graphics to highlight important features of the data and key points. Refrain from simply listing data and statistics. Interpret them and help people to understand what they mean. Use excerpts from young people's drawings and photographs to illustrate the findings, and use their exact words in quotations to highlight key points. Display data on maps when it makes sense to do so, highlighting the locations of favourite places, problem places, and other important community features and characteristics.

    Ideally, young project participants will be involved in the data analysis and can play a central role in organizing and presenting the results using their own words and images.

Use words and pictures as well as numbers to express key points. For example, children's drawings can be powerful in communicating their view of the area where they live. To the right is an example from the South African site of Growing Up in Cities. It was included as a representative example, along with several others, in a project report. The narrative is based on the child's own interpretation of her drawing, with some related information added by the project team member to help others understand and appreciate the information contained in the drawing.

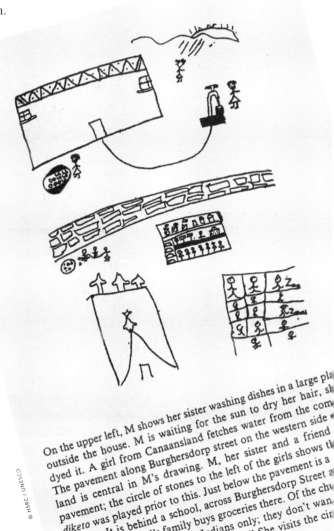

© HSRC / UNESCO

On the upper left, M shows her sister washing dishes in a large pla
outside the house. M is waiting for the sun to dry her hair, sh
dyed it. A girl from Canaansland fetches water from the com
The pavement along Burghersdorp street on the western side
land is central in M's drawing. M, her sister and a friend
pavement; the circle of stones to the left of the girls shows th
diketo was played prior to this. Just below the pavement is a
M likes. It is behind a school, across Burghersdorp Street a
                        ...it's for Indians only; they don't wan
                                    ...pelled." She visits the cir
                                                for this.

Planning for Change

The participatory evaluation of the local area will highlight a range of issues that need to be addressed. In most situations, there will be insufficient resources (money, people or time) to address all the key issues at once. Priorities must be set, a plan of action and schedule defined, and implementation activities funded, staffed and set in motion.

There is an almost endless list of possible actions that might be taken in response to any set of local issues. 'An action framework' on page 171 provides a basic structure for thinking about the different kinds of action that might be possible. The challenge is to

Young people in Melbourne, Australia, present their ideas for change to elected representatives and other community residents.

© KAREN MALONE

determine which actions will be the most effective given the issues and circumstances of the local area. It is rarely effective to adopt exactly the same action plan that proved successful elsewhere. Every situation is different, and requires a different response.

Developing an effective action plan involves four distinct steps — each of which should involve young people as active participants if not the actual leaders of the process.

1. **Define the issues to be addressed.** The initial step in the action-planning process is to identify the issues or problems that are the highest priority. Through a participatory process, local young people, adult residents, local decision-makers and other stakeholders should identify the priority issues or problems to address. The decision on the

Making prioritization fun

In the Growing Up in Cities site in Warsaw, Poland, the project team developed a game they called 'Dongs' to help young people to consider and prioritize their ideas for improving the local area. Each young person was given 100,000 'dongs' (an imaginary currency) and asked 'On what important projects for your neighbourhood would you spend it?' Each had to decide what projects they would like to focus on, and how much of their limited resources they would devote to them. Young people found the approach to be easy to understand and fun to do. Their individual 'investments' were then totalled to determine the group's rankings for investments, revealing their collective priorities for neighbourhood improvement.

action to take should be made strategically, taking into consideration available resources (including staff, volunteers, time and money) as well as the local situation, including the factors that create or affect the key issues and the relationships between key issues.

2. **Set goals.** This step often takes place in conjunction with identifying the priority issues, stating what the group wants to achieve in response to their priorities: their desired outcomes, in both the short and long term. Through an inclusive dialogue, the goal-setting process can be a very positive step in establishing a common agenda for the future, defining mutual aspirations and providing a powerful statement about what they want to collectively achieve (see 'Visioning' on page 168). Goal setting should also be strategic. The goals must respond to the identified issues, be realistic and achievable, and be grounded in political, social and economic reality.

'Hands-on' exploration of alternatives

Several of the Growing Up in Cities sites used three-dimensional models to help young people and other community members to explore ideas for improving their local area. In Oakland, California, a model was developed of the courtyard space that was young people's primary area for play and socializing. With movable model elements representing both existing and possible new features for the courtyard, young people and adult team members explored and evaluated different possibilities. The exercise was very popular with young people, and very useful for evaluating different design alternatives.

© ILARIA SALVADORI

3. **Explore alternatives.** In one form or another, participants need to consider alternative strategies, taking into consideration available tools and resources as well as potential opportunities and constraints. Participants should first develop a list of potential responses and strategies, and then explore each idea to understand its relative merits. All possible types of action should be considered (see page 171). Which actions will be the most difficult to implement? Which will be the most effective? What things can participants do themselves, and what must they rely on others to do for them? What can be achieved in the short term, and what will require a longer period of time? Through this participatory evaluation process — which may involve some technical input — participants will be able to define a set of strategies in response to community priorities.

4. **Develop an action plan.** Once a preferred course of action has been defined, participants should develop a strategic action plan, summarizing the key issues and goals and outlining the actions that have been devised in response. This represents the group's agreement for moving forward, and is therefore an important focal point for consensus building. The action plan should describe how the various actions and strategies will be implemented, including funding sources, responsible individuals or organizations, and

Developing community action plans by gender and generation

To articulate the needs of different groups within the community, it may be useful to develop ideas for action first in smaller groups, organized by age and/or gender. In this way, young people can express their issues and ideas separately from adults, and women separately from men. Then, once each group has developed a list of their issues and ideas, they can share between groups and develop a common plan for action that addresses concerns from all ages and genders. This approach has been used successfully in a number of places, including the Growing Up in Cities site in Johannesburg, South Africa.

a schedule. Ideally, it should include 'indicators' for measuring success and define the parameters of an ongoing monitoring programme (see page 175). The plan can be presented as a brief written document or summarized on large sheets of paper and posted in a place that all can see. Regardless of what form it takes, what is important is a common understanding of what the plan is, including who needs to do what, and when.

VISIONING

'Visioning' is a tool for identifying common values, building consensus and developing a comprehensive statement of what you hope to achieve.

A 'Vision Statement' describes what the community or project site (such as a park, neighbourhood or street area) will be like in the future — what it will look like, who will live there, what types of activities will take place there, etc. It is based on what participants think their community will be like once all the current issues are addressed. In other words, it is a statement of goals for the community's future, presented in a manner that is understandable to all. Individual projects and activities can then be evaluated against the vision to determine how effective they will be in making the vision a reality. The vision also provides a tool for monitoring success over time (see page 173).

The more people that are involved in the vision process, the more successful it will be. All members of the local community as well as decision-makers and other key stakeholders should have the opportunity to participate.

The basic steps in developing a vision statement include:

- **Brainstorm.** This gives everyone an opportunity to share his or her own vision and ideas about the future. It is a chance for all ideas to be heard — not for debating the merits of each vision or idea.

- **Identify common themes and shared values.** What do people's individual visions have in common? What ideas or images are mentioned most frequently? Are there any major differences of opinion? Work together to explore differences as well as common themes, trying to understand whether perceived differences are due to miscommunication, misperceptions, or fundamentally different ideas about the future.

- **Develop the vision.** Based on the common themes and shared values that emerge from the discussion, develop an initial description of the group's emerging vision. If possible, develop a sketch to give visual expression to the vision. Also, continue to explore ways in which different ideas about the future might be reconciled.

- **Articulate the vision.** Use words, sketches, diagrams, or whatever medium the group finds most effective to communicate the vision to other people. Some groups have described their visions for the future through stories (for example, 'a day in the life of…in the year 2020') or even short plays. The purpose of the vision is to express a set of common goals, to help the group to see their work in a long-term, 'big picture' perspective, and to stimulate others to join in making the vision a reality.

- **Revisit and update the vision.** Make sure the vision remains relevant by reviewing it periodically, thinking about new trends and developments in the local area as well as changes within the participating groups or organizations.

Envisioning 'the best place to live'

The South African site of Growing Up in Cities conducted a visioning exercise with young people through a drawing exercise. First, young people worked in groups to draw, on large sheets of paper, their images of the 'best place to live', describing the types of things they would want in an ideal community. The groups were then reorganized and asked to apply agreed-upon physical improvements to copies of a map of the local area. They shared the results of their work, laying out their 'visions' for how they might begin to create 'the best place to live' within the practical context of their local area.

Taking Action

Once the action plan is agreed upon, the challenge is to implement it successfully. The following guiding principles should be kept in mind when designing and implementing change-oriented activities:

© NILDA COSCO

Actions to improve the local environment can range from relatively simple, immediate activities like painting a local play space — as these children are doing — to more elaborate, long-term activities that seek to educate community residents or change development policies, as described on the following pages.

- **Maximize participation.** Identify the actions or changes that can be implemented by local residents using local resources and facilitate the participation of as many local residents as possible in making those changes. When outside resources are required, ensure that local residents play a role in determining how those resources are used and, to the fullest extent possible, in carrying out the related implementation activities.

- **Encourage youth action and leadership.** Encourage young people to take the lead in designing and implementing change-oriented actions. There may be some actions that young people develop and implement entirely on their own, and others where they provide the lead with assistance from adults, or still others where they work with adults as partners in the implementation and ongoing management processes.

- **Promote community-wide actions.** Implementation of the action plan can provide opportunities for involving local residents and institutions that may not have participated in earlier project activities.

- **Include actions for both short and long-term changes.** If all the actions will show results only in the long term, participants are likely to be disappointed with the slow rate at which change is occurring. On the other hand, if actions are oriented only towards short-term changes, the project's momentum may soon be lost.

- **Ensure visibility.** Contact representatives from the local media and encourage them to provide coverage of the project's implementation activities. This helps to develop widespread community interest and participation in the project, and can contribute to the sense of accomplishment and pride in the changes taking place.

- **Provide ongoing management.** Having talented and dedicated people to organize and coordinate ongoing implementation activities can be the most critical factor in ensuring success.

- **Develop a support network.** Throughout the project, look out for individuals and organizations that support the project's goals. They might provide valuable input, resources, or other forms of support to make change happen.

- **Facilitate reflection and evaluation.** Ongoing reflection and evaluation of the strengths/weaknesses and accomplishments/shortcomings of participation activities must be an integral part of the process.

An action framework

The type of change that is needed will vary according to the issue and the specific circumstances of the project and local area. Sometimes, the most important thing is to change people's attitudes about an issue. Other times, what is needed is immediate physical change in some aspect of the local environment. Most often, some combination of changes will be most effective in providing both short- and long-term solutions.

The following is a general overview of three different types of action that should be considered when developing a plan for making change happen.

PHYSICAL/ENVIRONMENTAL CHANGE ACTIONS

These are actions that seek to bring about some tangible change in the local environment, such as redevelopment of a public space or establishment of a new youth centre. These are very desirable types of action because local residents can see concrete results quickly and can often participate directly in making change happen.

An example of a physical/environmental change action is the 'Streetspace' project at the Growing Up in Cities site in Melbourne, Australia. The project was developed in response to the need identified by young people for a safe trail or pathway to enable them to cycle, walk or rollerblade to the neighbouring community, as well as find new points of interest along the way. Through the 'Streetspace' project, young people in a local secondary school were involved in a participatory design process, working with an environmental designer to develop a design for the pathway, as well as the renovation of a public green space that already had funding from the local municipality. The series of activities was structured to create a curriculum that future classes could follow to explore their area and plan community improvements.

Young people developed three-dimensional models to communicate their design ideas as part of the 'Streetspace' project.

© GUIC AUSTRALIA / M. FOOKE

A mobile environmental education unit — the Móvil Verde — in Buenos Aires, Argentina, helped implement a programme about 'the neighbourhood as a child's habitat' as part of the Growing Up in Cities project there.

© NILDA COSCO

EDUCATIVE/ATTITUDINAL CHANGE ACTIONS

These are actions that seek to raise the level of awareness about important issues or change the attitudes of local residents or the larger society. Examples of such actions include exhibitions of young people's writings, drawings or photographs; youth newsletters or poster campaigns; civic festivals or events; or development of a new school curriculum. Although results can sometimes be difficult to measure, they are the essential foundation for real, sustainable change in the local physical environment as well as in the larger social and political environments.

The Growing Up in Cities site in Buenos Aires, Argentina, implemented a variety of community actions that raised awareness about young people's perceptions of their local area and explored ways in which positive changes could be made. Activities included 'Gulliver's mapping' (see page 158), an exhibition of young people's photographs (see 'Our Neighbourhood Is Like That!' on page 133), and a series of design education workshops that involved children in implementing action projects in their neighbourhood. To carry out the various action components of the project, the team joined forces with a mobile environmental education unit (the Móvil Verde) of a local labour union organization.

The Mayor of Greater Johannesburg joined young people from the Growing Up in Cities site at a workshop focused on listening to their input and ideas and developing initial plans of action for moving forward.

© JILL SWART-KRUGER

POLITICAL/REGULATORY CHANGE ACTIONS

These are actions that seek to change the policy and institutional framework in which community development and decision-making take place. Examples of such actions include community organizing and mobilization campaigns around specific issues; voter registration; legislative actions; establishing youth councils; or establishing a 'youth ombudsman' or 'child advocate' in the local government. Changing the ways that government institutions operate and altering political power structures usually takes sustained, long-term effort. None the less, actions of this kind are often essential for achieving real improvements in the environment and quality of life for local residents.

The Growing Up in Cities team in South Africa approached the Mayor of Greater Johannesburg, while the participatory research with children was still underway, to ask him to participate in hearing the children's priorities once they were established. He generously agreed to host a workshop, which is described in greater detail on page 43 ('Multiple Levels of Participation in a South African Workshop'). The workshop provided a valuable opportunity for local young people as well as adults to learn more about their local politicians, legislators and bureaucrats. It was also an opportunity for them to voice their opinions and priorities directly to the decision-makers in attendance. The workshop also served to create and strengthen relationships between individuals and groups both within and without the local government structure who were concerned about local youth. This and other efforts by child advocates have borne fruit: the Mayor of Johannesburg is moving forward to make his city 'child-friendly', by actions such as the appointment of a member of staff to coordinate projects under this initiative.

Monitoring and Reflection

The process of participatory community development does not end with any single set of actions. It is a long-term process of community change and renewal. As part of that process, mechanisms for ongoing project monitoring need to be put in place, and opportunities for reflection and evaluation must be provided.

A participatory process of reflection and evaluation should occur not only at the end of every project, but also at key points throughout the process. This allows participants to consider the extent of their success, and to identify the barriers that are keeping them from being more successful. This can often point to structural and systemic issues that underlie many of the problems faced in local communities, particularly in lower-income urban communities. The reflection process thus becomes a consciousness-raising exercise that further contributes to the project's role as a vehicle for community awareness and empowerment. It may also lead to the reconsideration of goals, the redefinition of actions, the revision of strategies, or changes in the project's management or coordination.

Related to the need for regular reflection by participants is the need for an ongoing system of project monitoring, whereby indicators are regularly evaluated to document the project's progress towards meeting its goals. If the project monitoring shows that progress is not being made, this information can be incorporated into the group's regular evaluation activities, allowing participants to identify the possible reasons for the lack of progress and make adjustments to the action plan accordingly. Similarly, if the project monitoring shows that progress is being made and goals are being achieved, this will be valuable information for the community, providing a sense of accomplishment and allowing them to focus on subsequent steps in their action plan or to revisit key issues and focus on new areas of concern.

The following are guiding principles to keep in mind regarding project monitoring and reflection activities.

- **Reflect early and often.** Structure formal group reflection and evaluation activities into the planning process as well as the project monitoring process. Bring participants together at key points to reflect on their activities and accomplishments and discuss how to make the process more participatory and effective. Conduct brief reflection exercises at the end of each project activity or each project day. Make 'reflection' a daily habit rather than an end-of-project chore.

- **Provide a positive and supportive environment.** In all project activities, but especially evaluation activities, participants need to feel that their opinions matter and that they can say what they feel without risk.

- **Criticize constructively.** Start all evaluation activities by first discussing the good points. What went well? What have we achieved? Then discuss the potential weaknesses and areas of improvement. What could have gone better? What could be done differently to make the project more effective?

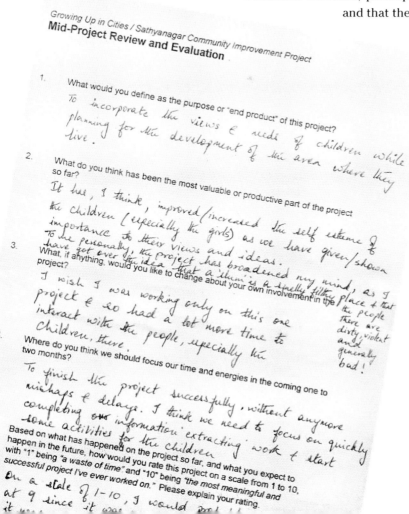

Example of an evaluation form used in the Growing Up in Cities site in Bangalore, India, to provide project staff an opportunity to give formal, written feedback part-way through the project. The individual written evaluations were followed by a group discussion to share reflections and explore ideas for responding to issues that had been raised.

- **Foster creativity.** There are many group process tools for engaging participants in reflection and evaluation. Role plays, drawings, interviews, and games can all be used to help people to think about what the project has achieved and how it could be done differently. Let participants develop their own reflection and evaluation tools, putting a different individual or team in charge of each group reflection session.

- **Establish indicators as part of the action plan.** 'Indicators' can be defined based on the goals of the action plan, providing a way to measure the project's success over time. Child-generated indicators of a good place in which to grow up, based on the results of the initial Growing Up in Cities research with young people, are summarized on pages 24 and 25 of this book, and discussed at greater length in the concluding chapter of *Growing Up in and Urbanising World* (see the Resource list in Appendix B). For purposes of monitoring the implementation of a project over time, indicators should be quantifiable. They should also be based on positive goals that the community is striving to achieve, rather than the negative factors it is trying to overcome (for example, 'the number of healthy trees in the neighbourhood' or 'the percentage of children attending school', rather than 'the levels of pollution' or 'the number of illiterate adults').

- **Accept criticism.** Encourage participants to look for some validity in every criticism and to try to understand the cause of the criticism. This may lead to greater appreciation of the diversity of perspectives among participants and to new insights on how to improve project activities.

- **Apply the lessons learned.** The lessons that come out of reflection and monitoring activities need to be documented and acted upon. Summarize the results of each reflection or monitoring activity, and follow up as necessary on any identified actions.

Involving young people in reflection and evaluation

Young people can be involved in the process of reflection and evaluation in many ways. In the South African GUIC site, children who had participated in the Mayor's Workshop (see page 43) were later shown a video of the workshop's proceedings and asked to talk about what they liked or did not like about the workshop. In all the sites, young people who were involved in the GUIC interviews were given an opportunity to talk about how they felt about being interviewed and the questions that were asked. Some sites also held small group discussions or interviews with child and youth participants to talk about what they liked and did not like about the project, and what they would do to improve it. Participants can also be given an opportunity to submit anonymous evaluation feedback in writing, or young people can conduct their evaluation discussion without any adult team members present, and then communicate the results of their group discussion to the project team.

Moving Forward

Creating better cities requires a long-term commitment to young people's participation in the community development process. Like adult residents of the community, young people should have real and meaningful opportunities to look at the area in which they live, identify opportunities for improving it, and act for change.

As was discussed in the early chapters of this manual, no participation process is ever perfect. There is always room for improvement. Similarly, no participation process can ever be fully replicated. Every place and point in time will present unique circumstances, each requiring a unique response. Lessons learned — positive or negative — should be constructively applied in subsequent projects.

As you gain practice and confidence in working with young people in participatory ways, you will develop new methods and approaches for encouraging greater participation. The young people you are working with will begin to take a more active role in facilitating the process and implementing change. If you are an adult, your own role may become less central, though none the less important, as you offer support to young people's initiatives and encourage them to ensure a participatory approach in their own dealings with their peers.

This manual is a tool for you to use in your efforts towards creating better cities with children and youth. Like any tool, it has its limitations and shortcomings. What matters most are the skills and commitment of the people who use it. There is no 'magic' in the methods and process guides. The magic lies in the people who make participation happen, and the human interactions that enlighten us, inspire us, and — in the end — provide the essential and lasting foundation on which better cities can be built.

Children from the GUIC project in South Africa enjoy the play and study centre they helped create. The centre is named *Ubuhle Buyeza* — IsiZulu for 'good things are about to happen'.

© JILL SWART-KRUGER

Data Collection Guidelines[1]

Census data, information on economic trends, maps of the area, historical photos and other types of descriptive data can provide a valuable comparison or juxtaposition to the information being generated by the participatory evaluation activities that are the focus of this manual. They can also inform the participatory planning process, helping residents to understand the local history, current conditions and future opportunities as well as revealing useful information that is critical to a successful plan of action. Ideally, this information should be collected throughout the participatory process, with young participants helping to define the data needs of the project and then collecting, compiling and analysing the available information.

The following is an overview of the types of data you may want to consider collecting. Not all the data listed will be needed for every project, and some additional types of specialized data may be needed for some projects. The intention here is to provide an overview. Review the 'Data collection checklist' on page 178 to determine which areas will be most useful to your project.

DATA COLLECTION OVERVIEW

Data collection should provide a comprehensive review and evaluation of information on your site's context, including its history, current conditions and trends.

While the data collection focuses on the local environment, it also takes into consideration conditions and trends in the larger environment that may affect the local area, such as regional or national economic trends, or the national political context. It provides base data for use in the participation process as well as for development of an action plan.

The scope and depth of your data collection will depend on your project's needs and resources. The 'Data collection checklist' (page 178) provides a quick overview of the types of information you may want to consider.

In addition to the guidance provided by the checklist, keep the following tips in mind as you undertake data-collection activities.

- **Allocate sufficient time.** Data collection can be very time-consuming, even in countries with extensive and accessible information networks. In some places, even basic data on the site's population can be difficult or impossible to obtain, either because it does not exist or is considered classified for political reasons. Do not assume that you can do the necessary data-gathering in the course of a couple of days or a week. It will probably require repeated inquiries, numerous trips and persistence. Allocate plenty of time, get started early and do not get discouraged when it takes longer than you thought it would.

- **Strive for complete, accurate data.** The roadblocks you encounter when seeking data on your site may cause you to settle for less than you had originally hoped for. Before you decide to do so, be sure that you have explored all possible avenues for finding relevant, meaningful data. If necessary, look at data that may be available for the larger population (extending

WORKSHEET

Data collection checklist

Following is a list of the types of background information and data you may need in the process of a community planning project. Use this list to determine the data items that will be most important for your project.

Columns: ESSENTIAL · DESIRABLE · NOT NEEDED

Maps
- [ ] [ ] [ ] Locational maps (global, national, regional, city, district)
- [ ] [ ] [ ] Base maps (of the entire project area or specific parts of it)
- [ ] [ ] [ ] Topographical map
- [ ] [ ] [ ] Land use map
- [ ] [ ] [ ] Figure-ground map
- [ ] [ ] [ ] Environmental resources map
- [ ] [ ] [ ] Community resources map
- [ ] [ ] [ ] Community design analysis map
- [ ] [ ] [ ] Traffic volume map
- [ ] [ ] [ ] Community infrastructure map
- [ ] [ ] [ ] Community hazards map

Photographs
- [ ] [ ] [ ] Aerial photographs
- [ ] [ ] [ ] Site photographs
- [ ] [ ] [ ] Photomontage (to show panoramic views)
- [ ] [ ] [ ] Process photographs
- [ ] [ ] [ ] Photographs taken by young people
- [ ] [ ] [ ] Visual survey or photogrid

Physical environment information
- [ ] [ ] [ ] Study area size
- [ ] [ ] [ ] Building types and conditions
- [ ] [ ] [ ] Sketches of typical home interiors
- [ ] [ ] [ ] Land use
- [ ] [ ] [ ] Transportation
- [ ] [ ] [ ] Public and civic spaces or facilities
- [ ] [ ] [ ] Open space and natural features
- [ ] [ ] [ ] Landmarks
- [ ] [ ] [ ] Urban services
- [ ] [ ] [ ] Relationship to adjacent areas, employment centres and city centre

- [ ] [ ] [ ] Environmental risks
- [ ] [ ] [ ] Environmental management and maintenance

Social and economic information
- [ ] [ ] [ ] Population and demographics
- [ ] [ ] [ ] Land tenure
- [ ] [ ] [ ] Cost of living
- [ ] [ ] [ ] Economic activity and indicators
- [ ] [ ] [ ] Child labour/youth employment
- [ ] [ ] [ ] Health status and services
- [ ] [ ] [ ] Education system and status
- [ ] [ ] [ ] Crime and safety
- [ ] [ ] [ ] Shopping and retail services
- [ ] [ ] [ ] Recreation and leisure

Political, legal and cultural information
- [ ] [ ] [ ] Political system
- [ ] [ ] [ ] Legal and regulatory context
- [ ] [ ] [ ] Municipal or local government
- [ ] [ ] [ ] Non-governmental organizations (NGOs)
- [ ] [ ] [ ] Activism
- [ ] [ ] [ ] Cultural and political attitudes towards young people
- [ ] [ ] [ ] Attitudes towards the environment
- [ ] [ ] [ ] Official policies about young people and the environment
- [ ] [ ] [ ] Official attitudes and policies about participation
- [ ] [ ] [ ] Recent or current proposals

Historical information
- [ ] [ ] [ ] Interviews and oral histories
- [ ] [ ] [ ] Historical documents
- [ ] [ ] [ ] Historical photographs

beyond your specific site), to provide at least some sense of the basic characteristics that may define residents of the area on which you are focusing.

- **Be cost-effective.** Be strategic in identifying the information that will be most useful. Do not collect more information than you will need and do not spend more time chasing data than is worthwhile. It is easy to fall into the trap of endless data collection. More information is not necessarily better information.

- **Explore non-traditional data sources.** Think creatively about possible sources of data about your site. In addition to the traditional sources such as government agencies and census publications, talk with non-governmental organizations and others that work in the area. They may have their own compilation of site data that will greatly enhance your efforts and perhaps save you a lot of time. Also check out local libraries, including university libraries, and tap into professional resources in your area. Local librarians, researchers, planners, architects and others will know where to look for data and will probably be more than happy to assist a good cause.

- **Document your sources.** Be sure to document the sources of your information, and to cite these sources whenever you refer to the information in documents or presentations.

- **Collect images as well as words and numbers.** Photographs, maps and other graphics are powerful tools for helping others to better understand the context of your research. They are also very useful for community discussions and other participation activities.

- **Differentiate between 'facts' and 'impressions'.** Be careful not to inadvertently mix 'facts' about your site with your own subjective 'impressions'. While your impressions are valuable, you must be sure to make it clear to the reader that such impressions are based on your own observation, and not on any statistical data or third-party information. Likewise, alert the reader to any potential shortfalls, unreliability or inconsistency in your data.

- **Maximize opportunities for participation.** Use the data-collection process as an opportunity for participation, helping to develop greater ownership and understanding of the data as well as beginning the process of looking more carefully and critically at the local environment.

OPPORTUNITIES FOR PARTICIPATION

Data-collection activities can be a great way for youth to get involved in 'hands on' project work and to learn more about the resources in their community. The act of going to the municipal planning office to obtain information on the local area can be very educational and eye-opening. Also, by collecting, compiling and mapping data, young people develop valuable skills and learn to look at their environment in new ways.

There are many ways to structure participatory activities around basic data-collection tasks. The feasibility of doing so will depend on the age and ability of the group, the extent and nature of the data being collected, and the time that the young people have to devote to such activities.

Some data-collection tasks may need to take place before the participation activities get under way (such as collecting maps or census information). Others may be best undertaken after the process has begun, involving young people in additional analysis on the key issues they have identified (such as compiling a visual survey or looking at local crime rates).

When undertaking a group data-collection exercise, be sure to follow some basic guidelines: clearly define individual and group responsibilities; establish firm deadlines; clearly label all data, maps and information; and maintain an organized filing system.

MAPS AND PHOTOGRAPHS

There are many different types of maps and photographs that may be useful. Those you decide upon will depend on the resources you have available and the unique needs of your project. The following is an overview of some of the more common map formats and types of photographs used in the planning and participation processes.

Maps

Maps are visual representations of geographical information. They can be extremely useful in the planning process when used properly, as well as extremely misleading when they are inaccurate, incomplete, poorly displayed or misused.

Maps can be useful for relating statistical information to the key ideas that arise from your interviews and interactions with young people. For example, if young people have complained that a particular street corner is very dangerous, it may be useful to develop a map of accidents that have been reported at the local police station. By mapping the location of accidents, culled from the pages of accident reports, you may provide valuable confirmation for what the young people have said, which can then support arguments for the need to make safety improvements. Alternatively, development of an 'accident reports map' may show a relatively low accident rate at the corner where young people feel unsafe, which may point to the need for different types of interventions — either to improve the accident reporting system (minor accidents involving pedestrians or bicycles may be going unreported), or to improve the perception of pedestrian safety at that intersection.

When using maps, be sure to consider the map-reading skills of project participants. If maps are unfamiliar, participants may find them intimidating. Consider using alternative forms of geographical representation that might be more familiar (aerial photographs, if available, are typically much easier to read

for most people). Or use this as an opportunity to develop participants' map-reading skills, giving time in the process for explaining how to read and use simple maps.

Following are brief overviews of some of the most common types of maps used in the planning process.

- **Locational maps.** These illustrate the location of your site within the surrounding area. They might include a global- or national-scale map, regional map, city map or neighbourhood map. They can be of great interest and educational value to young people.

- **Base maps.** A 'base map' is an outline drawing of an area on which you can then display a variety of geographical information, from the community's evaluation of the local environment (places they like best, places they like least, important landmarks, etc.) to information on issues such as land use and traffic. An example of a base map is given in Figure A-1. The map shows the basic street layout, buildings and key features in the local area. It does not contain too much detail or extra information that may make it confusing or difficult to read.

  A base map of your project area is extremely useful for describing the structure of the local environment and is essential to a planning project that will set forth recommendations for improvements in the local area. It provides a uniform, consistent format for discussing the community's environmental perceptions and evaluation results.

  As for all maps, the base map should include a scale and a compass arrow helping to orient the user. Also, make sure that it can be reproduced clearly in black and white.

  You may want to consider having several different scales of base map covering different parts of your site. For example, an *area map* covers the whole of your project area as well as nearby features that are identified by the community as being of importance in their daily lives. Depending on the size of your site, you may find it useful to have this map in

FIGURE A-1

Base map

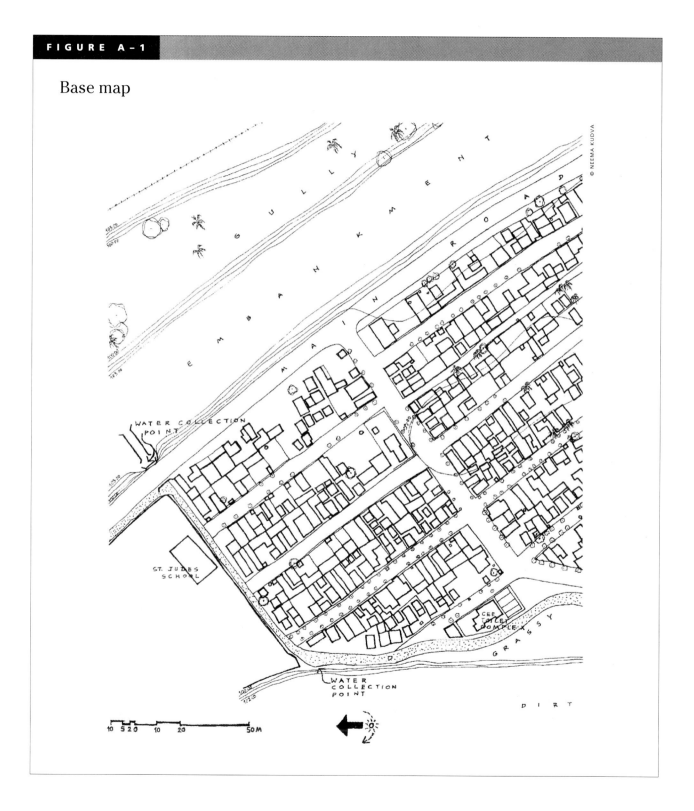

the 1:1000 to 1:2000 scale range. To 'zoom in' and explore particular areas or features of your project site, you may also want to have a *block-level map* or *detail area map*. This may be necessary if you have a large or complex site or if, through the participatory process, you have decided to focus on one particular part of the larger area. These maps are typically in the scale range 1:100 to 1:500.

- **Topographical map.** Another type of base map is a topographical map. It shows the elevations and contours of the land at your site. If you have a site where topography plays a key role in the way the community uses or perceives the environment (e.g. it has

steep hills), this will be a valuable map to have. If the information is not too complicated, you may want to incorporate topographical information on your site base map. But if the addition of topographical lines makes the base map hard to read, then keep the information on a separate map. The sample base map in Figure A-1 includes contour lines showing every one-foot change in elevation. The contour lines are most noticeable in the change of elevation between the Main Road and the embankment (where there is an increase in elevation), and between the embankment and the gully (where the elevation drops once again).

- **Informational maps.** Once you have a base map, you can use it to develop informational maps that illustrate different aspects of the site's characteristics and use. These kinds of map provide valuable opportunities for participation, with young people examining the local environment to document different types of information and then displaying that information on the base map. The following are some examples of mapped information that is often collected in community planning processes.

  > *Land use map* identifying the general types of land activities at your site (homes, shops, offices, industrial sites, parks, schools, etc.). By filling in each parcel or building with a colour that indicates its use, you may begin to see patterns emerge that you had not noticed before. You can also use the map to indicate other important characteristics such as the height of buildings or types of housing. Figure A-2 shows an example of a land use map.

  > *Figure-ground map* to help in understanding the pattern of built and unbuilt spaces in an area (see Figure A-3). The term 'figure-ground' is used to describe the way in which we perceive an image, with the 'figure' being the image that our eye tends to focus on, and the 'ground' being everything else. The artist M.C. Escher is well-known for his explorations of figure-ground drawings, in which the

About map scales

The 'scale' of a map indicates the relationship between the size of the map and the size of the actual area that it portrays. A map that is 1:1000 scale indicates that every unit on the map equals 1000 units on the ground. In countries that use the metric system, this means that 1 centimetre of distance on the map is equal to 1,000 centimetres (or 10 metres) on the ground. Therefore, on an A4 (21 cm by 29.7 cm) sheet of paper, a map drawn at 1:100 scale would reflect an area of approximately 180 metres by 250 metres (assuming space for margins and a caption). If the same map were drawn at 1:1000 scale on the same sheet of paper, it could reflect an area of approximately 1.8 kilometres by 2.5 kilometres.

In addition to identifying the scale of a map as a ratio, it is also useful to express it visually. That way, when a map is enlarged or reduced using a photocopier or other device, the scale will be enlarged or reduced as well. Figure A-1 shows an example of a visual scale in the lower left corner.

Note on map scales in the United States. In the USA, where the metric system has yet to catch on, units of map measurement are typically expressed in terms of '1 inch equals "XX" feet or '1 inch equals "XX" miles'. Because of this, it is important to state the units being used on the map and, ideally, to provide a visual scale as well.

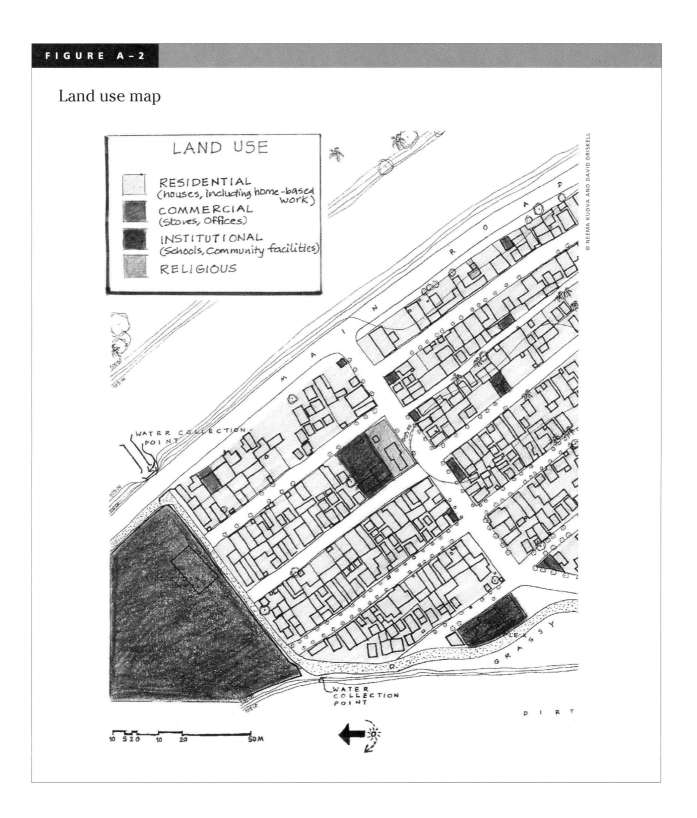

FIGURE A–3

Figure-ground map

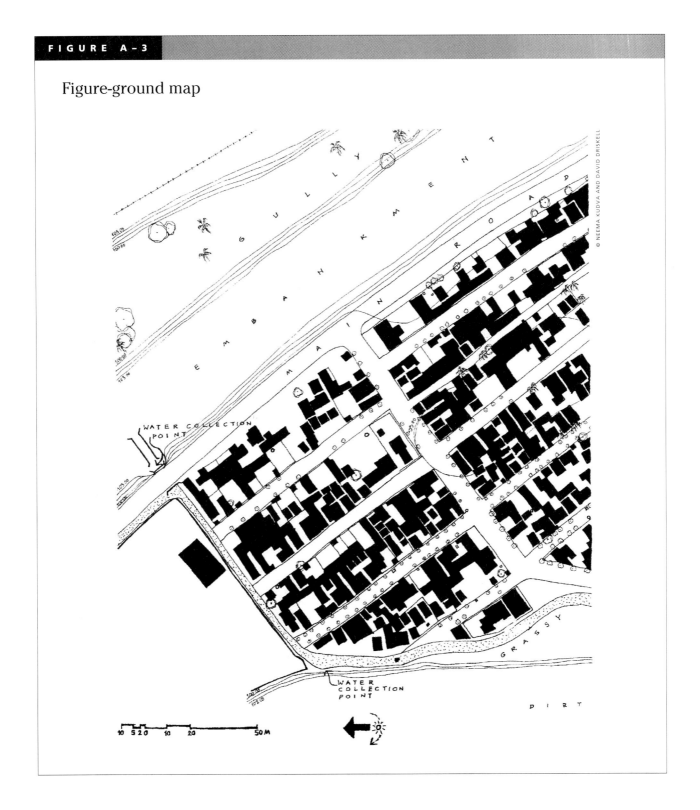

viewer perceives different images depending on whether he focuses on the dark areas of the image (the figure) or the white areas (the ground). In a figure-ground map, all the buildings are coloured solid black, and the areas that are not built are left white. The result is a clear, graphic statement about the community's pattern of development and both the amount and configuration of remaining open spaces (whether public or private).

> **Environmental resources map** to show the location of important environmental resources, such as trees, open spaces, hills, watercourses or areas of vegetation. This map can also be used to highlight environmental issues in the community (such as a polluted stream or a rubbish dump).

> **Community resources map** to identify the resources in the local area that are valued by community members. These might include recreational resources (parks, open spaces, trails); religious institutions (churches, mosques, temples); government facilities (municipal buildings, libraries, community centres); or child-oriented facilities (schools, daycare centres, playgrounds). It might also include places where people meet, such as a local market or coffee house; bus stops or railway stations; or places that have a special significance or meaning for the community (a monument or historic site).

> **Community design analysis map** to provide a graphic representation of the visual and functional form of the local environment, reflecting how people use and perceive the local area (see Figure A-4). This should be developed based upon observation of how people use the local area as well as upon input from project participants. A group mapping of the local area's community design can be a valuable group-learning experience. Elements that might be displayed on this type of map include districts or neighbourhoods (larger areas that have a common identity or use); gateways (important entry points to

the local area or district); pathways (major routes of movement through the area); nodes or activity centres; landmarks (major features that people use to orient themselves in the site area); and edges (the physical or perceptual boundaries that separate one area or district from the next).[2]

> **Traffic volume map** to illustrate the level of vehicular traffic on roads passing through or near the site. Data on traffic volumes can sometimes be obtained from the local planning or transportation authority, and may help to shed light on the environmental conditions faced by young people at the site. If such data are not available, they can be developed easily through simple traffic surveys, counting the number of passing vehicles at various times of the day and week. Traffic data can then be displayed on the base map using different colours or thicknesses of lines to represent different volumes of traffic.

> **Community infrastructure map** to illustrate the locations and extent of basic services in the local area. It might illustrate areas that are without running water or electricity; show the locations of major utilities (e.g. electricity lines or water mains); show the locations of features such as street lamps and water hydrants; show the locations of bus or rail services; or identify major utilities such as power sub-stations or sewage treatment plants.

> **Community hazards map** to identify issues in the local environment that pose potential health and safety hazards to community residents. These might include rubbish dumps, open drains, toxic sites, deteriorating buildings, dangerous road crossings or areas of high crime. Identification of these issues can be based on the community's perceptions and experiences as well as data gathered from local authorities (for example, mapping the locations of violent crime during the past year might reveal a clear pattern of hazardous places within the community).

FIGURE A–4

Community design analysis map

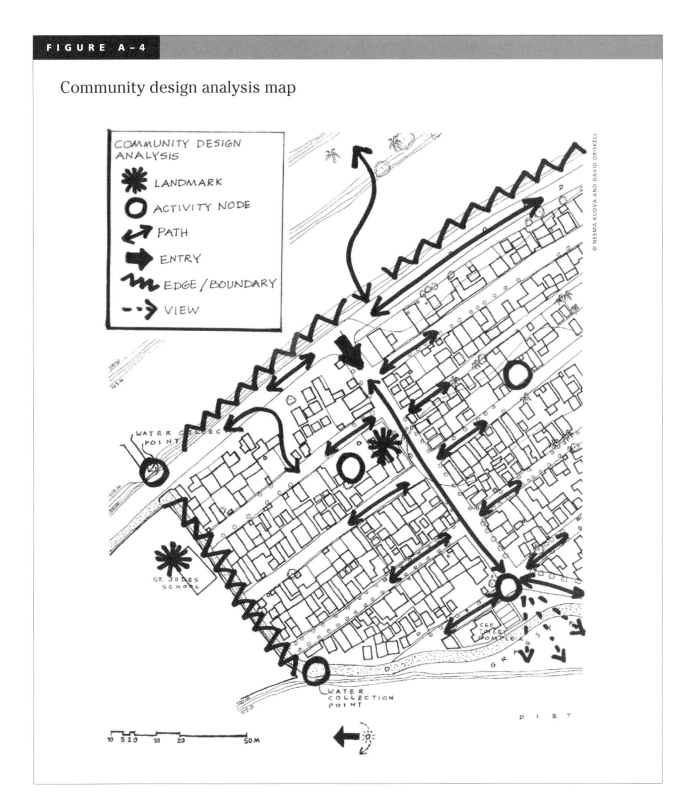

Aerial photographs

An aerial photograph is extremely useful for showing the site's location, layout and (to a certain extent) physical qualities. It is also a useful participatory planning tool. People of all ages enjoy seeing aerial photos of the places they live, and most young people will be able to quickly and easily read and understand them. In particular, enlargements of aerial photos (which can simply be photocopied by sections onto pieces of paper and taped together) can be very useful for making annotations about the site and conducting small-group discussions.

Aerial photos are often shot in a grid format, with each photograph overlapping with the next photograph in the grid. Such photos may be available from the local planning agency, municipality or regional authority, though these offices may charge a fee to provide copies. In some countries, aerial photography from satellites is available on-line or from private agencies.

These are usually of sufficient resolution for exploring large areas, but may be inadequate when working in smaller, block-sized areas.

A time-series of aerial photos (showing the site at different points in time) can be extremely useful for showing historical changes in the site's physical size and character, and for stimulating community discussions about those changes.

An example of an aerial photograph is shown on page 108.

Photographs

Photographs are an invaluable tool for documenting the local environment, stimulating community discussion and communicating your project area's characteristics to others.

Photographs taken by young people can be an effective participation method (see page 130). They can also be used to document the use of public spaces in

Finding maps and aerial photographs

In some places, access to mapped information is widespread, with a variety of new digital formats easily available on-line. In other places, accurate up-to-date maps are much more difficult to obtain, making it necessary to develop your own base map for your site.

The following are suggestions of the type of place you may want to look to find maps of your area:

- Local urban planning office, transportation department or municipal development authority
- Local university library, geography department or planning department
- Public library or historical society/archive
- The Internet (full of surprises)
- Local bookstore
- Local non-governmental organization or community-based organization that does work — especially development work — in your area
- Military/space agency or geographical survey office
- Local developer's office or planning consultant's office

If you are unable to locate a suitable map, then you may need to develop one on your own. This can be done by enlarging and adding to a portion of a larger area map (e.g. a map of the city) or by taking information from an aerial photograph (if available). Or it may require making a physical survey of the local area and developing a map based on the survey data. If it is necessary to develop your own map, try to find an architect, planner or cartographer with mapping or drafting experience to help prepare it. They will have experience in drawing plans to scale and can produce a fairly accurate map. Another source of technical assistance in preparing maps of your site might be the urban planning, architecture or geography department of a nearby university.

Conducting a Visual Survey or Photogrid

The purpose of a visual survey or photogrid is to systematically document — in photographs — the physical character of the local area. It can provide valuable information on the local environment for use in public discussions and in explaining the local area to people outside the community, helping them to quickly understand its visual quality, characteristics and important features. Photographs can also be a valuable source of historical information for future community residents.

Following are directions for conducting a visual survey.

- **Gather the necessary materials.** To conduct a visual survey and properly archive its results you will need:
  (1) copy of your site map or aerial photo
  (2) pencil and tracing paper
  (3) colour print film
  (4) camera

- **Determine the interval you will take photos.** The basic idea is to take photographs of the area at regular distances. A 100 metre interval is suggested, but this may need to be modified based on the constraints or characteristics of your site. There is no exact number of photos that you will need — this will vary depending on the size of the area. You should strive to provide a complete sense of the physical character and quality of the entire project area.

- **Draw a grid and overlay it on the site map or aerial photo.** Draw the grid, based on the interval you selected, on a transparency or tracing paper, and lay it over your map. The location of each grid intersection is where you will take a photo. Shift the grid as necessary so that the grid intersections fall in accessible locations (for example, orient the photogrid in the same direction as your site's street grid). Mark the location of each grid intersection on the map or aerial photo.

- **Take a photograph showing a view of your site from each grid intersection.** Using the map you have marked, take a colour-print photo showing a characteristic view of your site from an accessible outdoor space that is at or close to each grid intersection, such as the nearest street, yard or other public place.

- **Choose views or features that are important to children.** In general, the purpose is to take photos that will provide as complete a picture as possible of your site's environment (both perceived strengths and perceived weaknesses). Specifically, be on the lookout for young people engaged in activities, or environmental features that are related to young people's activities (for example, barriers, territorial markings or user modifications).

- **Take additional photographs as necessary.** Take as many pictures as are necessary to explain special features of your site or to describe in detail elements that have proved to be important to children's behaviour. This may require taking more than one photo from a single grid intersection, or from points outside your regular grid.

- **Record the location and perspective of each photo on the map or aerial photograph.** Mark the exact location and perspective of each photo taken; and reference each photo to the grid using an alpha-numeric system, with each row of the grid identified with a letter and each column identified with a number. A photo with the reference 'C12' would be taken at the grid mark where row 'C' and column '12' intersect.

- **Catalogue and archive negatives and prints.** Create a 'Visual survey binder' that includes (a) the site map or aerial photo on which you marked the locations and references of the photos; (b) the prints and/or contact sheets of the photos; and (c) the negatives. Be sure that all photographs and negatives are labelled with the date and location, and properly stored (see page 94, 'Keeping things organized').

FIGURE A-5

Photogrid

The map indicates the location of each photograph that was taken, while the photographs themselves are displayed according to their location on the grid.

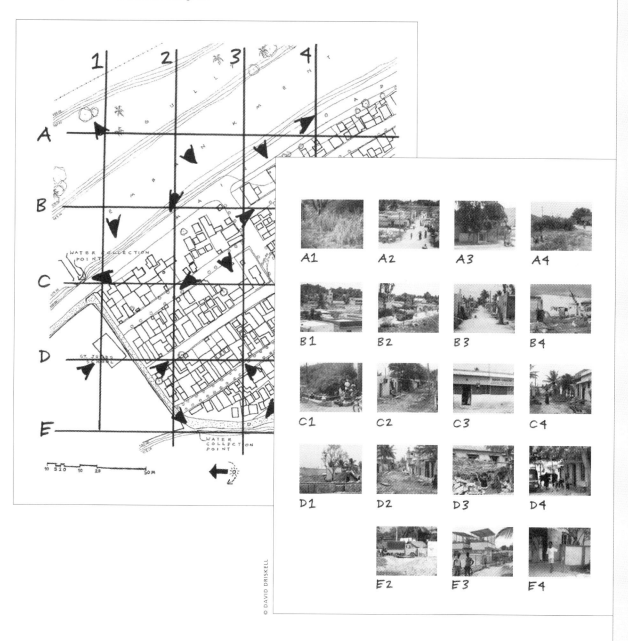

© DAVID DRISKELL

the local area. Be sure to use photographs to document your planning process and participation activities. This is particularly important if you plan to use the process as a pilot project for replication in other sites or if you will need to explain the process to funding agencies, government officials or others outside the local area.

Remember that an image paints a thousand words, and that one photograph can communicate many important messages about a place or activity. However, like any language, you need to be careful how you use and interpret photography. Do not think only of what is in any particular photo, but also about what is not in it. Are your photographs giving an accurate description of the place? Are you leaving out important information or images by not including them?

PHYSICAL ENVIRONMENT INFORMATION

In addition to maps and photographs, you will want other types of data and information about your site. You should start collecting this information early in the research process to provide a more complete understanding of the site. While the specific information you will want to include will vary, the following list provides an overview of things you may want to consider when studying the site's physical qualities.

- **Study area size.** Document the overall size of the site, including the size of any important features (for example, the width of a main road or the area of a central plaza). Be consistent in the measure that you use (square metres, hectares, acres, square miles) so that it will be easy to make comparisons later.

- **Building types and conditions.** What forms of housing do people live in? What are the general building and plot sizes in the area? How tall are the buildings? What types of materials are used? What are the architectural styles? How well are the buildings maintained?

- **Sketches of typical home interiors.** What types of housing do people live in? What are the typical sizes

of a dwelling and its rooms? How many people live in a single dwelling unit? What are typical furnishings and amenities? How are the different rooms of the house used? This information can be documented in simple freehand sketches showing the layout of the house, drawn roughly to scale, supplemented by written notes. Photographs can also be included, but only if they can be taken without disturbance. If you are working with older children, they can be asked to develop sketches of their own homes, complete with notes describing each room and how it is used. Or interviews with parents may afford an opportunity for collecting this information, but only if it does not distract from the interview and is not perceived as an intrusion into family privacy.

- **Land use.** How much of the site is used for residential purposes? Are there businesses or industries located within or adjacent to the site? What are they, and who uses them? How much of the land in the site is dedicated to streets and other car-oriented uses? Are there any other major land uses in or adjacent to the site (schools, military sites, large institutions)? Where do most people do their daily shopping? Are there any temporary land uses, such as spaces occupied on a routine basis by street vendors and carts, a weekly market or an annual festival? Map this information as appropriate on a land use map of the area, supplemented by photos or written descriptions.

- **Transportation.** What types of vehicular and pedestrian traffic exist on the site? Are there various types and speeds of vehicular transportation on the site ranging from hand-pulled rickshaws or bicycles to fast-moving lorries and cars? What types of public transportation serve the site? How frequent is the service, and where does it go? How do most people who live at the site get to work or go shopping? What are the most heavily trafficked streets? What is the level of car ownership in the area? How much traffic is travelling to or from the site versus travelling *through* the site?

- **Public and civic spaces or facilities.** Are there any significant public facilities in or adjacent to the site, such as a large plaza, school, library, church, government office or community centre? How many people go there on a typical day? What types of activity take place there? Does it serve only a particular age or income group, or does it serve everyone? Does it serve people from all over, or just people from the site? Are special events or festivals held there at any time during the year? How are streets and open spaces of the city transformed during special events and festivals?

- **Open space and natural features.** What is the general ratio of 'built' space to 'open' space in the site? What type of open space is it? What condition is it in? Is it accessible? Who uses it? Are there any significant natural features in or adjacent to the site (river, lake, tall tree, grove of trees, field, etc.)?

- **Landmarks.** What are the site's most prominent built features (either within the site or visible from the site)? Are these recognized as landmarks by both local residents and visitors? Are there social, cultural and historical landmarks in the site that may not be evident to visitors? Who owns or maintains the site's most important landmarks?

- **Urban services.** Is the site serviced by all major utilities (electricity, water, telephone, sewage, sanitation)? Who owns and maintains these services? Are there any pressing infrastructure problems (power shortages, potholes, standing water, etc.)?

- **Relationship to adjacent areas, employment centres and city centre.** How easy is it to get from the site to adjacent areas? What are those areas like? Are they similar to the one being studied? Do people from that area come to this one, and vice versa? Where is the nearest employment centre? How do people get there? How close is the site to the city centre?

- **Environmental risks.** Are there any records of air, water or soil pollution? Does municipal or industrial dumping present a hazard for children at play? Are there any industrial activities, transport facilities or other activities in the local area that are major sources of pollution or pose other significant risks to children?

- **Environmental maintenance and management.** Who is responsible for maintaining and managing the local environment? Is there evidence of informal systems of environmental maintenance or management by local residents?

SOCIAL AND ECONOMIC INFORMATION

You will also want information on the site's general social and economic conditions. The following are some of the types of information you may want to consider.

- **Population and demographics.** It is sometimes difficult to obtain an accurate population count and breakdowns of demographic information. However, an estimate of the population's size and basic demographics is helpful. To develop a realistic estimate, draw on your own or others' observations, data for the larger area, or estimates provided by a service agency working at the site. You should also try to find historical data or other information that will shed light on how the site's population has changed in recent years.

  Demographic categories that you should try to cover include age, gender, income, religion, race/ethnicity, caste/class, home ownership/rental, education and occupation. Compare this information with citywide statistics to understand how the site relates to the city as a whole.

- **Land tenure.** One issue of major importance in many low-income settlement areas is whether or not the local residents own the land on which they live or, at a minimum, have legal, secure rental or lease agreements. If residents do not feel secure in their legal right to remain in an area for the long term, it will probably be reflected in their level of investment in the area (financial as well as emotional).

- **Cost of living.** What are the typical housing costs in the area? How much do people pay for food? How much do they spend on education, health care, transportation and other necessities? How much do they spend on leisure and recreation? How do these costs compare with the typical family income?

- **Economic activity and indicators.** What are the main occupations and business activities for people at the site? How far do parents commute? Are there informal business activities that people engage in? How many hours do people work in a typical day? What is the status of the municipal, regional or national economy? What are the recent and current trends?

- **Child labour/youth employment.** Do children or youth participate, formally or informally, in the local economy? At what age do people start work? What role do children and youth play in helping to meet household expenses? Is the role different for boys and girls? If children or youth are working, what sort of work are they doing, for how many hours, and in what sort of conditions? Who do they work for and how much do they get paid? Do they have a say in how the money is spent? Are legal protection and services available to them? Are they aware of such protection and services? Once children or youth start working, are they able to continue with their schooling in some form?

- **Health status and services.** Are any statistics available regarding the health of the site's population (infant mortality rate, incidence of infection or disease, life expectancy, etc.)? Is there a health clinic or hospital within the site or close by?

- **Education system and status.** What is the structure of the local education system and what is the focus of its curriculum? At what age do children typically start and finish their schooling? How many children go on to further schooling, in or outside the community? What is the drop-out rate? Are there differences based on gender of the child? Are there alternative schooling systems? What is the literacy rate among adults? What forms of education or technical training are available for adults? Who controls the local school, both in terms of curriculum and facilities? How involved are local parents in the schooling of their children? How do children get to school? Are the schools considered to be safe?

- **Crime and safety.** Do people generally feel safe and secure in the local area? Is there a sense that the local crime rate is disproportionately high? Do young people feel safe moving about the area on their own? Is there a cooperative relationship with the local police department? Are some parts of the area considered worse than others in terms of crime and safety? Is there a sense that things are getting worse or better? How do people's perceptions of crime and safety compare with local statistics, if any? Are these statistics considered to be reliable?

- **Cultural facilities and programmes.** Are there any cultural facilities located within the local area or nearby? Do young people participate in cultural activities, formally or informally? Are they familiar with cultural institutions in the city (museums, libraries, concert halls, etc.)? Do they visit those facilities or participate in their programmes? If not, why not? Are there differences between boys and girls?

- **Shopping and retail services.** Where do people shop? How do they get there? When do they go? Where do young people go to shop? Are these places easy to reach on their own? Do they feel welcome there? Are there gender differences in where or when young people shop?

- **Recreation and leisure.** Where do people in the community go for recreation and leisure? Are there places within the community or do they have to travel elsewhere? How much time do they spend in a typical week in recreation and leisure activities? Do different age groups or socio-economic groups tend to spend recreation and leisure time together or apart?

POLITICAL, LEGAL AND CULTURAL INFORMATION

Information that helps to shed light on the site's political and cultural context and official attitudes towards young people, environment and development issues will be important, particularly when discussing possible actions that may be defined through the participatory process. If you are conducting interviews with local officials, you are likely to gain many relevant insights. However, you may also want to conduct some basic background research about the following issue areas.

- **Political system.** What is the form of government nationally, regionally and locally? How is the local population represented? Who has power in making decisions that affect the people and environment at your site? What is the general level of public awareness of and involvement in the political process? To what extent do the elected representatives reflect the overall composition of the community they represent?

- **Legal and regulatory context.** What laws and regulations shape the local planning and development processes? Are there mechanisms for enforcing local laws and regulations regarding planning and land development? Is there an established legal framework for children's rights and community participation?

- **Municipal or local government.** Which municipal departments are responsible for issues related to children, youth and the environment? Which departments oversee planning and land-development decisions? Which departments have been most active in the local area? Is there a history of cooperation between the local community and the municipal or local government? Who do the departments report to? What are the attitudes of local residents towards the municipality, and vice versa?

- **Non-governmental organizations (NGOs).** Do non-governmental organizations work in the local area? Are there groups focusing solely on issues related to children, youth, the environment or planning and development? Do these groups have a history of working together or an established mechanism for collaboration? Is there a positive working relationship between local NGOs and the municipality? What are the attitudes of local residents towards these NGOs, and vice versa?

- **Activism.** Are there any signs of political organization and activism among the residents? Who is responsible for organizing them? What are the issues around which they have organized and taken action? What forms of action do they take? How successful are they? Do young people ever participate in these actions?

- **Cultural and political attitudes towards young people.** How are children and youth treated within the local culture or subculture? What are the general attitudes towards their development? What is considered 'proper behaviour' for young people? How do attitudes towards boys and girls compare? This information can emerge from interviews with parents and officials; from documentation from standard sociological or anthropological studies; or from local novels, tales, songs, news clippings, jokes or drawings. In gathering this material, be sure to note the various sources, remembering that a community is a collection of diverse subgroups, each expressing its own ideas and attitudes. Be on the lookout for differences between subgroups (possibly based on factors such as gender, age, caste/class, and cultural background).

- **Attitudes towards the environment.** Consider how the use of public spaces or general attitudes about the environment shape young people's opportunities and experiences in their community. Are there signs of local 'stewardship' or environmental activism (clean-up or recycling programmes, protected open spaces, a community garden, well-tended public spaces, etc.)? Is any form of environmental curriculum taught in the local schools? Do people generally know the names of indigenous plants and animals?

- **Official policies about young people and the environment.** What are the official policies that directly influence the local physical environment of young people? How long have these policies been in effect? Are they enforced? Have there been any previous efforts to change these policies? Is there any reference to the needs of children and youth in local policies regarding development, planning or environmental management? Are there any local policies regarding children's rights?

- **Official attitudes and policies about participation.** Is there a history of participatory planning in the area? Is there an openness or enthusiasm from local officials towards ideas of participation?

- **Recent or current proposals.** Are there any proposals that have recently been put forward, or are currently under consideration, which will change or affect the local environment (new policy directions, major new developments, etc.)?

HISTORICAL INFORMATION

It is often illuminating to explore the historical conditions that have shaped development in the local area, particularly major trends or events that may have resulted in significant changes or added new features to the current environment.

- **Interviews and oral histories.** For recent events, relevant pieces of site history may come to light during interactions with young people ('there used to be a large area here to play, but then they put up this office building…'). For events further back in time, it can be illuminating to conduct interviews with older members of the community. If young people help to conduct these interviews, they will have an excellent opportunity to learn about their community's history, and create intergenerational links between young and old community members at the same time.

- **Historical documents.** A search in the local public library, university library or historical archive may reveal historical documents or books that shed light on the history of the site. This too can be an excellent opportunity to involve young people in the hands-on research process. They can be asked to explore different aspects of their community's history, or document the history of their own family and how they came to live in the area (extending the site's history into a broader social history of the community).

- **Historical photographs.** A valuable stimulant for community discussion can be a display of historical photos or maps showing change in the community (or one part of the community) over time. An aerial or panoramic view showing the community at various intervals in the past will attract people's attention and spark numerous discussions of how the place has changed, for better or for worse.

ENDNOTES

1 The information in this section draws upon a number of sources, including the 'graphics guidebook' that was developed for use in the 1996/97 Growing Up in Cities project sites by Beau Beza of the Melbourne, Australia, team, with assistance from Robin Moore and Nilda Cosco of the Buenos Aires, Argentina, team.

2 Kevin Lynch, the original project leader for Growing Up in Cities in the 1970s, wrote a book entitled *The Image of the City* (MIT Press, 1960) which remains a classic urban-planning text. It lays out a language for talking about and analysing the visual and functional form of urban areas, and incorporating input and perceptions from the people who live in these areas. It is a highly recommended resource for groups that want to develop a community design analysis of their area.

Resources

Following is a list of resources that may be useful in conducting a participatory community development project with young people. *This is not an exhaustive list of resources!* It is likely that there are other resources available in your local area or region of the world. One of the advantages of involving people with different backgrounds and areas of knowledge in your project team is that they will know of other resources that are available locally. Consult with a local librarian or faculty in a nearby college or university to get their ideas and input. Examples of academic departments or disciplines to contact include Anthropology, Sociology, Urban Planning, Architecture, Youth and Family Studies, and Environmental Education. If you have access to the Internet, you may also want to do a search for organizations in your area that are interested in community development, participation, or issues related to children and youth. The list of Internet links at the end of this section can provide a starting point for your search.

BOOKS ON PARTICIPATORY THEORY AND METHODS

Building Community: a tool kit for youth and adults in charting assets and creating change

Innovation Center for Community and Youth Development
2001. ISBN 0-9712642-0-1

This facilitators' handbook was created to enable individuals and groups to bring an inclusive, asset-based approach to creating positive change in their community. The handbook is filled with detailed information and case studies to lead users through activities for creating youth-adult partnerships for community development.

Internet: www.theinnovationcenter.org/product.asp

Changing Places: children's participation in environmental planning

Eileen Adams and Sue Ingham. 1998. ISBN 1 899783 00 8

A book for planners, architects, landscape architects, community and youth workers, and teachers, about how to engage young people in the process of planning for change, both through changing attitudes towards the environment and changing the environment itself. It provides a framework to enable professionals to involve children in planning their physical environments, and includes 20 detailed case studies from the UK.

Published by The Children's Society (London).
Fax: +44 0171-841-4500; Internet: www.the-childrens-society.org.uk

Children's Participation: the theory and practice of involving young citizens in community development and environmental care

Roger A. Hart. 1997. ISBN 1-853833-22-3

A comprehensive look at the theory and practice of children's participation in community development, with a rich variety of case examples ranging from data collection and evaluation to implementation and ongoing environmental management by young people. It argues that all children can play a central role in sustainable development if their participation is taken seriously and if communities recognize their developing competencies and unique strengths. The case studies draw upon examples in urban and rural, poor and middle-class communities in both the developed and developing worlds. The book introduces organizing principles and conceptual issues, successful models, practical techniques and resources for involving young people in environmental projects, with useful further reading and contact addresses.

Published by Earthscan Publications, Ltd. (London) with UNICEF (New York). Internet: www.earthscan.co.uk

Children as Fellow Citizens: participation and commitment

Micha de Winter. 1997. ISBN 1-857751-79-5

Written for professionals in youth and social policy, social services, health care, education, and social science, this book observes that young people are typically excluded from significant decision-making in their schools and communities, but suddenly expected to show civic awareness and commitment as soon as they reach adulthood. The real foundation for citizenship, it argues, are social experiences in responsibility and commitment from a young age. With a European emphasis, the book presents many examples of ways to involve children actively in different arena of their communities, including local planning, education and youth care.

Published by Radcliffe Medical Press (Oxford and New York). Internet: www.radcliffe-oxford.com

Cities for Children: children's rights, poverty and urban management

Sheridan Bartlett, Roger Hart, David Satterthwaite, Ximena de la Barra and Alfredo Missair. 1999. ISBN 1-853834-70-X

Cities for Children is intended to help urban authorities and organizations understand and respond to the rights and requirements of children and adolescents. It looks at the responsibilities that authorities face, and discusses practical measures for meeting their obligations in the context of limited resources and multiple demands. While the book emphasizes the challenges faced by local government, it also contains information that would be useful to any group working to make urban areas better places for children, including ways to educate children about their rights and involve them in democratic processes.

Published by Earthscan Publications, Ltd. (London) with UNICEF (New York). Internet: www.earthscan.co.uk

Environmental Education for Empowerment: action research and community problem solving

William Stapp, Arjen Wals and Sheri Stankorb. 1996. ISBN 0-7872-2341-7

This manual was developed for use by international programs linked through GREEN, the Global Rivers Environmental Education Network. With an emphasis on school models of action-oriented education, the manual gives step-by-step examples of how students, teachers and administrators can work together to plan, implement and evaluate action on numerous issues that affect local sustainability.

Published by Kendall/Hunt Publishing (Dubuque, IA, USA). Internet: www.kendallhunt.com; Email: orders@kendallhunt.com

The Facilitator's Guide to Participatory Decision Making

Sam Kaner, with Lenny Lind, Duane Berger, Catherine Toldi and Sarah Fisk. 1996. ISBN 0-86571-347-2

This is a 'how-to' manual for participatory group decision-making. It covers the mechanics of group decision-making, from developing meeting agendas to reaching closure. It is not written specifically for working with young people, although the approach it sets forth may be useful to those for whom facilitation and group decision-making is new. The authors state that the manual is intended for organizations and facilitators of all kinds — 'from board rooms to activist groups.'

Published by New Society Publishers (Blaine, WA, USA). Internet: www.newsociety.com

Growing Up in Canaansland

Jill Swart-Kruger, editor. 2000. ISBN 0-7969-1907-0

This report describes participatory research methods used with children aged 10 through 14 from the Canaansland squatter camp, and discusses the results. It outlines the children's preparations for the Mayor's workshop to share findings with urban planners, and summarizes workshop deliberations. In the process, the report serves as a detailed guide to organizing an event of this kind. The subsequent, unexpected relocation of Canaansland to a desolate spot outside the city is recorded, and a petition lodged in protest is reproduced. An epilogue contains the children's reflections.

Published by On the Dot Distribution. Internet: www.hsrc.ac.za (click on 'publications').

Growing Up in Cities: studies of the spatial environment of adolescence in Cracow, Melbourne, Mexico City, Salta, Toluca, and Warszawa

Kevin Lynch, editor; from the reports of Tridib Banerjee, Antonio Battro and Eduardo Ellis, Peter Downton, Maria Susulowska and Tadeusz Tomaszewski.

1977. ISBN 0-262-12078-X and 92-3-101443-9

This book summarizes the process and results from the original 'Growing Up in Cities' project of the 1970s. Although out of print, it is available in many university libraries, and provides an excellent historical perspective on the Growing Up in Cities project, which was one of the first cross-cultural explorations of young people's perceptions of the urban environment.

Out of print. Originally published by the MIT Press (Cambridge, MA, USA) and UNESCO (Paris).

Growing Up in an Urbanising World

Louise Chawla, editor.

2002. ISBN 92-3-103817-6 AND 1-85383-828-4

This book explores the relationship of young people to their urban surroundings in eight countries, focusing on low-income neighbourhoods in both the developing and developed worlds. It is the sequel to the pioneering Growing Up in Cities project conducted over 20 years ago, and a companion volume to this manual, as several of its case studies show the benefits that follow from the active participation of young people in the planning and implementation of urban improvements. Written by an interdisciplinary team, the chapters are enlivened with examples, maps, photographs, and drawings.

Published by UNESCO Publishing (Paris) with Earthscan Publications, Ltd. (London). Internet: www.unesco.org/publishing and www.earthscan.co.uk

The Kid's Guide to Social Action: how to solve the social problems you choose — and turn creative thinking into positive action

Barbara A. Lewis. 1998 (REVISED EDITION). ISBN 1-57542-038-4

Designed for use by youth age 10 and up (with a strong US orientation), this workbook covers the skills, resources, and tools needed to achieve social and environmental justice goals. It first identifies specific projects and then takes young people through steps such as letter writing, Internet research, interviewing, speeches, surveys, petitions, fundraising, media coverage, campaigning, voter registration, and protesting. Short vignettes illustrate how techniques have been successfully used by young people. The book also explains local, state and national law-making, political lobbying, the court system, and conflict resolution. It includes samples, reproducible worksheets, and resource listings including many websites.

Published by Free Spirit Publishing, Inc. (Minneapolis, USA). Internet: www.freespirit.com

The Participation Rights of the Child: rights and responsibilities in family and society

Målfrid Grude Flekkøy and Natalie Hevener Kaufman.
1997. ISBN 1-85302-490-2

Written by the world's first Ombudsman for Children and a scholar of international human rights law, this book reviews the legal basis for children's rights, including their rights of self-expression and participation. It provides practical examples from many different cultures of ways to consider children's self-expression, focusing on children in everyday situations in their families and institutions, in the context of their evolving capacities from birth to adulthood.

Published by Jessica Kingsley Publishers (London, UK).
Internet: www.jkp.com

PLA Notes (Notes on Participatory Learning and Action)

The principal aim of 'Notes on Participatory Learning and Action' is to enable practitioners of participation throughout the world to share their field experiences, conceptual reflections and methodological innovations. The series is informal and seeks to publish frank accounts, address issues of practical and immediate value, encourage innovation, and act as a 'voice from the field.' Distributed in February, June and October. Of particular note are their special issues that have been published on 'Participatory Tools and Methods in Urban Areas' (Number 21), 'Children's Participation' (Number 25), and 'Children's Participation — evaluating effectiveness' (Number 42).

Published by the International Institute for Environment and Development, Sustainable Agriculture Programme in London, UK. Internet: www.iied.org; publication ordering: www.earthprint.com

Planning for Real

Neighbourhood Initiatives Foundation (UK).

NIF is a national charity in the UK (Telford, Shropshire) specialising in community participation, training and development. They have developed a participatory planning approach that they term 'Planning for Real.' Working with local community networks, and using tools such as large-scale maps and three-dimensional models, community members explore local issues and potential responses to those issues, leading to development of an Action Plan.

A variety of materials related to 'Planning for Real' are available from NIF (UK). Tel: +44 (0) 0870 770 0339;
Fax: +44 (0) 01952 591 771; Internet: www.nifonline.org.uk

Planning with Children for Better Communities: the challenge to professionals

Claire Freeman, Paul Henderson, and Jane Kettle.
1999. ISBN 1-861341-88-1

This book is intended for local planners and policy-makers, municipal agencies, children's rights officers, youth workers, play workers, and other groups or organizations that play a role in local decision-making, community development and youth services. Written primarily for a UK audience, it clarifies why children's participation should be prioritised, using case studies from a variety of professions and disciplines to explain different methods to support participation.

Published by Policy Press, Bristol, UK. Internet: www.bris.ac.uk/Publications/TPP/tpp.htm

Stepping Forward: children and young people's participation in the development process

Victoria Johnson, Edda Ivan-Smith, Gill Gordon, Pat Pridmore and Patta Scott, editors. 1998. ISBN 1-85339-448-3

Stepping Forward evolved from an international workshop on children's participation held by the Institute of Development Studies, The Institute of Education, and Save the Children UK in September 1997. The book provides an overview of key issues and challenges facing those facilitating children's and young people's participation. It was based on the input of workshop participants, which included development NGOs, children's agencies, academic institutions and governments in the UK, Eastern Europe, Asia, Africa, the Caribbean and Central and North America. It includes a rich variety of case studies organized around key themes, such as ethical dilemmas, process and methods, and children's participation in crisis situations.

Published by Intermediate Technology Publications (London, UK). Tel +44 0171 436 9761; Fax +44 0171 436 2013; E-mail: orders@itpubs.org.uk; Internet: www.itdgpublishing.org.uk

Youth Participation in Community Planning

Ramona K. Mullahey, Yve Susskind, and Barry Checkoway. PLANNING ADVISORY SERVICE REPORT NUMBER 486. 1999. ISBN 1-884829-32-5

This manual is intended for North American planners who want to create an ongoing community youth involvement program. It focuses on three types of programs: land use planning, social activism, and policy making, and details the elements needed to develop a youth involvement project, including organizational structure, required resources, suggested activities, and hoped-for accomplishments, as well as some of the stumbling blocks. In-depth case studies show how seven cities in the United States and Canada have established effective youth programs, overcome obstacles, and achieved results.

Published by the American Planning Association (Chicago, USA). Tel: 1-312-786-6344; Fax: 1-312-431-9985; Internet: www.planning.org

Youth Planning Charrettes: a manual for planners, teachers and youth advocates

Bruce Race and Carolyn Torma. 1998. ISBN 1-884829-19-8

Youth Planning Charrettes provides guidance for preparing workshops and 'charrettes' — in which youth participants develop their own solutions to real-world problems, usually related to community planning and urban design problems. Case studies illustrate the process throughout the book. There are work-sheets, sample assignments, and step-by-step instructions for adult facilitators. The manual is targeted to adults, especially city planners and community organizers in North America, who want to involve youth in projects being implemented by adult groups or city governments.

Published by APA Planners Press (Chicago, USA). Tel: 1 312 786 6344; Fax: 1 312 431 9985; Internet: www.planning.org

The Youth Power Guide: how to make your community better

Urban Places Project, University of Massachusetts, Amherst, USA. 2000. ISBN 1-892893-01-0

This 'how-to' guide is based on the experiences of a youth-oriented community development program in Holyoke, Massachusetts, USA. It is written for use in an after-school setting by young people aged 10 to 19 and contains ideas and activities for developing a neighbourhood improvement plan, although it can be used for smaller projects as well. Activities range from 'Deciding on Your Purpose' and 'Brainstorming a Vision of Your Ideal Community,' to 'Getting Community Input and Support' and 'Doing the Project.' It is written for use by youth peer leaders and the adults who work with them, focusing on youth as the driving force behind the process, giving them tools to be able to improve their physical environment and to realize that they can be effective agents of change.

Published by the UMass Extension, University of Massachusetts (Amherst, Massachusetts, USA). Tel: 1 413 545 2717; Fax: 1 413 545 5174; Internet: www.umass.edu/umext/bookstore

RESEARCH GUIDES

Basics of Qualitative Research: techniques and procedures for developing grounded theory

Anselm Strauss and Juliet Corbin.
1998 (2ND EDITION). ISBN 0-803959-40-0

The second edition of this widely used text presents methods for analysing and interpreting qualitative data. Although set within a more traditional research framework (this is not a participatory or action-research text), it does provide a useful guide for structuring and analysing qualitative data, including how to code and analyse data and report the results. It provides definitions and illustrative examples, and presents criteria for evaluating a study as well as responses to common questions posed by students of qualitative research.

Published by Sage Publishing (Thousand Oaks (CA), USA; London, and New Delhi). Internet: www.sagepub.com, or www.indiasage.com

Children in Focus: a manual for participatory research with children

Jo Boyden and Judith Ennew, editors. 1997.

This training manual provides a comprehensive overview of children-focused participatory research methods. It is designed for use in conducting method training, and includes overviews of important background discussions, tools for both classroom and field-based learning about participatory research methods, and an overview of how to compile, analyse and present results. It is primarily intended for programme and project staff in child-oriented non-governmental organizations (NGOs) and research institutions, but will be useful to anyone who is conducting participatory research activities with young people.

Published by Rädda Barnen (Save the Children) Publishing (Stockholm). Fax: +46 8 698 90 14; E-mail: rbpublishing@rb.se; Internet: www.childrightsbookshop.org

Fieldwork with Children

Robyn M. Holmes. 1998. ISBN 0-761907-55-6

This is one of the few qualitative research guides focused specifically on fieldwork with children. It explores fieldwork with children from a number of perspectives, and helps to address the needs of researchers working with children. It includes an overview of the study of children and discusses basic methodologies, and concludes with a discussion of how a researcher's personal attributes, such as gender and ethnicity, affect research with children.

Published by Sage Publishing (Thousand Oaks (CA), USA; London, and New Delhi). Internet: www.sagepub.com, or www.indiasage.com

Introduction to Action Research: social research for social change

Davydd J. Greenwood and Morten Levin.
1998. ISBN 0-7619-1676-8

Introduction to Action Research is geared towards researchers and practitioners who are interested in the history, methods and potential application of Action Research (AR) in their work. It introduces the history, philosophy, social change agenda, methodologies, ethical arguments, and fieldwork tools of AR. It uses case studies drawn from the authors' own practice, including some examples of failures. In the final section of the book the authors cover six different approaches to doing AR.

Published by Sage Publications, Inc. (Thousand Oaks (CA), USA; London, and New Delhi). Internet: www.sagepub.com, or www.indiasage.com

Participatory Action Research

William Foote Whyte, editor. 1991. ISBN 0803937431

This book provides a comprehensive introduction to Participatory Action Research (PAR). It takes the reader step-by-step through PAR as a research technique, from the initial design of a project, through data gathering and analysis, to final conclusions and actions arising out of the research. The authors outline the theory and methods behind PAR, weigh its strengths and weaknesses, then present a series of case studies. Although the book is not directly linked to issues of community development in urban areas, or to the application of PAR with young people, it is a useful text for people who would like a more thorough grounding in the approach and methods of PAR.

Published by Sage Publications, Inc. (Thousand Oaks (CA), USA; London, and New Delhi). Internet www.sagepub.com, or www.indiasage.com

Research with Children: perspectives and practices

Pia Christensen and Alison James, editors.
2000. ISBN 0-203-02460-5

This book is a collection of chapters by authors from different academic disciplines who have used children as researchers or spokespeople in studies of different aspects of their lives, including education, health care, and social welfare programs. The authors reflect on the methodological, practical and ethical dimensions of this work.

Published by Falmer Press (London, UK).
Internet: www.tandf.co.uk

A Trainer's Guide for Participatory Learning and Action

Jules N. Pretty, Irene Guijt, Ian Scoones, and John Thompson; Illustrations by Regina Faul-Doyle.
1995. ISBN 1-899825-00-2

A guide for training others in the use of 'Participatory Rural Appraisal' (PRA) techniques, including researchers, practitioners, policy-makers, villagers and other trainers. Although PRA methods are designed for use in rural areas with adults, most can be easily adapted for urban areas, and many can also be adapted for use with young people. The manual is valuable both in providing a description of methods as well as providing a useful training tool, with ideas for energizing the group, encouraging reflection, and preparing for fieldwork.

Published as part of the 'IIED Participatory Methodology Series' by the International Institute for Environment and Development, Sustainable Agriculture Programme (London).
Internet: www.iied.org; publication ordering: www.earthprint.com

UNITED NATIONS POLICY DOCUMENTS

Convention on the Rights of the Child

United Nations Children's Fund (UNICEF). 1989.

The Convention on the Rights of the Child (CRC) is an international human rights treaty that establishes children's fundamental freedoms and the inherent rights of all human beings. The CRC has been ratified by nearly all Member States of the United Nations and therefore has legal status in most countries.

A pamphlet on the CRC can be downloaded free of charge from the UNICEF website, at http://www.unicef.org/CRCpamphlet/ pamphlet.htm. Additional resources pertaining to the CRC can be found on the UNICEF website (www.unicef.org)

The Habitat Agenda

United Nations Human Settlements Programme (UN-Habitat). 1996.

The 'Habitat Agenda' was the outcome of the Habitat II 'City Summit' in Istanbul, emphasizing the need for governments to involve young people in participatory community development processes.

The full text of the Habitat Agenda and related information regarding its implementation can be accessed online at www.unhabitat.org

Agenda 21

United Nations Conference on Environment and Development (UNCED). 1992.

Agenda 21, the Rio Declaration on Environment and Development, was adopted by more than 178 Governments at the United Nations Conference on Environment and Development (UNCED) in 1992. Children and youth were identified as major groups who must be involved in the processes of sustainable development and environmental improvement.

The text of Agenda 21 and related information regarding sustainable development can be accessed online at www.un.org/esa/sustdev/agenda21.htm

VIDEOS

Children of Thula Mntwana: growing up in cities

UNESCO and Jill Kruger Research. 2001.

Children describe and evaluate their lives in Thula Mntwana, a squatter camp in Johannesburg, South Africa. The principal character, 13-year-old Zukiswa, explains how her family became squatters in Braamfontein through force of circumstance. She tells of how she and other children in the squatter camp then learned through the Growing Up in Cities project to identify problems in their living community, how they presented insights to public officials, and the resources that they gained from the project. Nevertheless, they continue to struggle in an inhospitable environment.

Available from UNESCO Publishing, Tel +33 1 45 68 4930; Fax +33 1 45 68 5737. Internet: www.unesco.org/publishing

Growing Up in Cities: partners in research and planning

Jill Swart-Kruger

Produced by the Growing Up in Cities team in South Africa, this video provides information and visuals on the project site and edited footage of the workshop hosted by the Mayor of Greater Johannesburg, at which children from the Growing Up in Cities site presented their viewpoints to urban officials.

Available from Unisa Press (Pretoria, South Africa). Tel: +27 12 429-3448; Fax: +27 12 429-3221; E-mail: unisa-press@unisa.ac.za

Mirrors of Ourselves: tools of democratic reflection for groups of children and youth

Roger Hart and Selim Iltus

This video is designed for use by groups of children or youth that are reasonably self-organized. It provides an introduction to how children, youth, and their facilitators can assess the democratic qualities of their organization and reflect critically on its structure and their decision-making processes in order to improve them. The methods include: social maps, comparative benefits charts, card sorting, activity preference matrices, diagrams of political structure and political influence, and drama. The methods are illustrated by video, followed by colour animations to give the viewer a clear, step-by-step description of each method.

Available from Save the Children Alliance, Kathmandu, Nepal, or from the Children's Environments Research Group, Graduate Center of the City University of New York. Internet: www.reddbarna.no (Save the Children Norway) or www.cerg1.org (Children's Environments Research Group). Email: post@savechildren-norway.org.np (Save the Children Norway in Nepal).

INTERNET RESOURCES

The Internet is an ever-expanding resource covering a wide range of topics. Because it is constantly changing, it is difficult to compile a list of Internet resources for print with any assurance that it will remain useful over time. Never the less, the websites below can be used to get started on a search of useful online information resources.

At the Table

www.atthetable.org

This initiative of the Innovation Center for Community and Youth Development is an online clearinghouse of resources and information for youth voices and involvement in their communities. It enables adult facilitators and youth themselves to connect with others, share information and find out about useful resources and events. The site is sponsored by the National 4-H Council of the United States, with a US focus, but its scope is worldwide and includes urban as well as rural programmes.

Child Rights Information Network

www.crin.org

The Child Rights Information Network (CRIN) provides information and networking for groups working for children's rights. Their website includes extensive resource listings, including publications, email lists, and regional information on partner organizations working to promote children's rights in Africa, Asia, the Americas, Europe, the Middle East and Oceania.

Childwatch International Research Network

www.childwatch.uio.no

The Childwatch International Research Network is a non-profit, non-governmental network of institutions involved in research for children. They help coordinate research and information projects on children's living conditions and the implementation of children's rights. They were one of the early sponsors of the Growing Up in Cities project. Their network of 'Key Institutions' around the world may be helpful in identifying potential institutional partners for local initiatives.

Growing Up in Cities / UNESCO MOST Programme

www.unesco.org/most/guic/guicmain.htm

The Growing Up in Cities website provides information on the project's history, publications, partners and various country sites, including contact information for the various country teams and the international coordinator. The site is hosted by the MOST Programme of UNESCO, the primary sponsor of the Growing Up in Cities project.

Institute for Development Studies (IDS) — Participation Group

www.ids.ac.uk

IDS, at the University of Sussex (UK), is a centre for research, innovation and learning in citizen participation and participatory approaches to development. While much of its work has focused on rural development issues, many of its resources and programmes are applicable to work in urban areas as well. Its website provides a variety of information resources, including on-line documents as well as for-sale publications and videos. It also provides an overview of current programmes and initiatives, and links to related websites.

International Institute for Environment and Development (IIED)

www.iied.org

IIED is an independent, non-profit organization headquartered in London that promotes sustainable and participatory development through research, communication and engagement with stakeholders at various levels. Its website provides an overview of its research network and publications, many of which focus on issues related to young people, participatory planning, and development.

International Institute for Sustainable Development (IISD)

www.iisd.org

This website has the complete text of the 'Youth Sourcebook on Sustainable Development' *(www.iisd.org/youth/ysbk000.htm)* which was developed by an international working group to support implementation of Agenda 21. It contains case studies of youth action, advice for organizing youth participation projects around environmental issues, and an extensive listing of international and regional youth organizations.

International Save the Children Alliance

www.savethechildren.net

Save the Children is one of the oldest and largest international NGOs focusing on issues related to young people and development. Their website provides an overview of their programmes and partner organizations throughout the world. The Save the Children sites in the UK *(www.savethechildren.org.uk)* and Sweden *(www.childrightsbookshop.org)* provide online catalogues and ordering information for their many publications.

International Secretariat for Child Friendly Cities

www.childfriendlycities.org

The Child Friendly Cities Initiative (CFCI) was launched in 1996 as an outcome of the World Conference on Human Settlements (Habitat II) resolution to make cities liveable places for all, with the well-being of children as the ultimate indicator of a healthy habitat, a democratic society and good governance. The International Secretariat for Child Friendly Cities — established by UNICEF, UNCHS (Habitat), the Italian Committee for UNICEF and the Istituto degli Innocenti — provides information and support to interested municipalities with the key objective of sharing experiences and encouraging networking among cities committed to improving the quality of life for their children and fulfilling their rights.

International Youth Foundation

www.iyfnet.org

The International Youth Foundation (IYF) is an international non-governmental organization that supports programmes serving children and youth. They work with national foundations and organizations in 45 countries. Their website lists their partner organizations as well as programmes they have identified as being effective.

UNICEF Innocenti Research Centre

www.unicef-icdc.org

The Innocenti Research Centre (IRC) is the main research arm of UNICEF. Based in Florence, Italy, it serves as an information resource centre in support of the implementation of the Convention on the Rights of the Child and the Child Friendly Cities Programme (see website entry for the 'International Secretariat for Child Friendly Cities').

United Nations Development Programme (UNDP)– Civil Society Organizations and Participation Programme

www.undp.org/csopp/cso

The website for the Civil Society Organizations and Participation Programme (CSOPP) of UNDP provides information about the unit's operations as well as information for Civil Society Organizations (CSOs) working in support of Sustainable Human Development. The site provides a list of programmes, partners and a resource centre.

United Nations Human Settlements Programme (UN-Habitat)

www.unhabitat.org

UN-Habitat is the lead agency within the United Nations for coordinating activities in the field of human settlements. It is the focal point for implementation of the Habitat Agenda, with an overall emphasis on reducing poverty and promoting sustainable development within the context of a rapidly urbanizing world. Its website provides an overview of its mission and programmes as well as related resources.

YouthActionNet

www.youthactionnet.org

This site was initiated by the International Youth Foundation as a 'virtual space' where young people can share lessons, stories, information and advice on how to lead effective change. It also provides information and resources to support participatory, youth-led action.

Index

Index compiled by Indexing Specialists, 202 Church Road,
Hove, East Sussex BN3 2DJ United Kingdom